D0952870

COMMODITIES TRADING

THE ESSENTIAL PRIMER

COMMODITIES TRADING
THE ESSENTIAL PRIMER

Russell R. Wasendorf
with
Pat Stahl

DOW JONES-IRWIN   Homewood, Illinois   60430

ISBN 0-87094-292-1

Library of Congress Catalog Card No. 84-72289

Printed in the United States of America

1 2 3 4 5 6 7 8 9 0 B 2 1 0 9 8 7 6 5

PREFACE

In all the years I've been involved in futures trading I have found very few basic books. There are many books that explore the complexities of commodity trading, but few that explain the operations of the market; hence, prospective commodity traders are usually left to their own devices to learn how the market works. This can be a time-consuming—and costly—process. My experience as a trainer for investors and brokers has taught me that the time devoted to learning the rudiments of futures trading is well spent: It lays the foundation for an ever-increasing knowledge of futures trading.

This book is designed to provide a cornerstone in that foundation. It gives beginning investors an overview of a dynamic industry—its origins, its operations, and its rules—while enabling experienced traders to polish their techniques.

The text is divided into four parts. The first part discusses the evolution of the current futures marketplace, and the second outlines technical and fundamental market analysis techniques. Part Three reviews the internal and external regulations that govern the industry, and Part Four offers practical suggestions for trading profitably in futures markets.

Beginning investors tend to have the greatest difficulty understanding the principles of hedging in the futures market and the regulations that govern the industry, so these concerns are covered at some length.

Whether you're a seasoned trader or a beginning investor, this book will arm you with the theory and the strategic tools you need to function effectively in the futures market.

Russell R. Wasendorf

CONTENTS

COMMODITIES TRADING

TRADING

THE ESSENTIAL PRIMER

PART ONE

INTRODUCTION TO THE FUTURES MARKET

Introduction

Economic historians have found evidence that merchants and producers in 2000 B.C. China were using principles of commodity futures in their contractual agreements for the delivery of commodities. Rice producers would agree to contract with merchants to supply a specific quantity of rice at a future date. It was not uncommon for the contract to be made prior to the actual planting of the rice. Merchant and producer negotiated a price for the future delivery of the rice and established that price as a part of the agreement. This contractual agreement assured the merchant that at harvest time a specific quantity of rice would be available at a predetermined price. The rice producer was assured of a market for the crop at an agreeable price. The principles of this agreement are the essentials of the modern futures contract.

Part One of this text will explore how the modern futures market evolved from these ancient trading procedures, how risk is controlled in the futures marketplace, and why exchanges and clearinghouses were established.

1

THE HISTORICAL FOUNDATION OF THE FUTURES MARKETS

The Emergence of Chicago as a Trade Center

It was not until almost 4,000 years later, in the early 1800s, that commodity futures contracts evolved into the important financial vehicle that they are today. Chicago, the heart of the nation's richest farmlands, was at the center of this development. During the nineteenth century, Chicago's commodity futures and agriculture grew together because the city was able to meet basic marketing needs of both agricultural producers and grain merchants.

The Seasonal Surplus to Shortage Problem

At harvest each year, farmers hauled to town the grain they would not need for their own consumption. Chicago became a natural basin for this excess grain. During harvest, a time of surpluses, grain users pressed for low prices, often forcing farmers to sell at distressed prices.

Buyers stockpiled as much grain as they could afford at low harvest prices, but storage facilities were scarce. As the year progressed, the supply of stored grain shrank and users were forced to bid aggressively for the remaining supply still stored on farms. Thus began the annual cycle of surpluses to shortages. Violent price swings from harvest lows to late season highs drove the grain industry to search out an alternative marketing method—forward contracts.

Forward Contracts

A Useful Marketing Tool

To secure a steady grain supply, users sought out farmers who would agree to contract grain for delivery at regular intervals throughout the year. Fearing the low prices of harvest sales, farmers willingly entered such agreements. The early contracts were tailored to a particular buyer and seller. They specifically stated the price, quality, quantity, delivery date, and location of each delivery. By contracting with grain users, farmers knew in advance the price of the grain they would deliver at a future date. Contracting also gave the users the comfort of knowing they would have grain when they needed it.

The art of securing a contract for the future delivery of grain became known as forward contracting. The term *forward* refers to a date forward in time. Forward contracts, sometimes called *to arrive contracts,* were narrowly specified to fit the exact needs of the buyer and seller. Buyers and sellers of these contracts gave personal guarantees of performance. In fact, the buyer often paid the seller a portion of the stated value of the grain.

Once the farmer had inked in a forward contract, he removed the risk of a price decline. The price stated in the contract was exactly what he could expect for his grain on delivery day. At least one risk remained for the farmer: a drought or crop spoilage might prevent him from making good on the quantity or quality of grain for delivery. In this case he would be forced to buy grain to fulfill the commitment—at times a costly option.

The user was similarly bound by the contract, but in this case the danger was more likely to be price. If the grain price declined unexpectedly, the user might not be able to take full advantage of a reduced input cost; he would have to pay the higher contract price.

Despite these pitfalls, the advantages of the forward contracts definitely made them useful in the balance. Actually, they have stood time's test well. Even today, most farmers fix prices before delivery through forward contracts.

In summary, a forward contract between the buyer and the seller of a commodity is an agreement with specific terms. The terms of the forward contract include the specific quantity and grade of a specific commodity to be delivered to a specific location at a specific future time. In drawing up the contract, the buyer and seller agree to the price of the commodity.

A forward contract between a corn merchant and a corn producer would include the following specific terms:

10,000 bushels of No. 2 yellow corn to be delivered to Des Moines, Iowa on October lst for $3.12 per bushel.

The forward contract is likely to include various other terms such as default clauses and special legal statements.

Inadequacies of Forward Contracts

Forward contracts suffer from an inherent problem: they lack flexibility. To understand the limitations of forward contracts, consider the following situation:

The date is July 15. A farmer has 100 acres of crop land planted with corn. The crop seems healthy, and the farmer is expecting it to yield 100 bushels of corn per acre or a total production of 10,000 bushels.

On the same date, July 15, a corn oil refiner examines his inventory and finds he needs 10,000 bushels by harvest time to meet his oil production goals.

If, on July 15, the farmer feels confident that he will have 10,000 bushels of corn to deliver at harvest, he may want to find a buyer willing to set the price of the grain to be delivered in the future. If the corn oil refiner is sure that he will need 10,000 bushels at harvest time, then he may seek to lock in a price for that input cost. Similarly, the refiner may want to find a seller willing to contract for a future delivery.

As the corn buyer and the seller bargain, they hammer out specifics of a forward contract. They agree upon price, let us say $3.25; quality, No. 2 yellow corn; quantity, 10,000 bushels; delivery place, at the refiner's factory; and time of delivery, Oct 10. The seller signs the contract, obligating himself to accept delivery. If the price of corn declined during the contract period, the seller would be protected but the buyer would lose the opportunity of buying at a lower price. If the price rose, the buyer would enjoy the lower input cost but the seller would lose the opportunity to sell at a higher price.

Suppose that after signing the forward contract the corn farmer experiences a major crop failure that reduces his production to only 5,000 bushels. The forward contract obligates him to deliver 10,000 bushels, so the farmer would have to purchase corn in the cash corn market to satisfy the contract, thus compounding his already severe loss.

A similar problem could arise for the refiner if a decline in the value of corn oil were to dictate a reduction in output. Because the refiner would be contractually bound to accept delivery of 10,000 bushels of corn, a portion of this corn would have to be sold in the open market due to production cutbacks.

The forward contract was an improvement over producing and holding grain in the hopes of higher prices, but it still proved to be an inefficient and inflexible way to market a crop when supply or demand changed unexpectedly. Grain marketers needed a mechanism that would transfer price risks to someone else.

Development of Contract Standards

As forward contracts became more common, speculators appeared on the scene hoping to make a profit by assuming temporary buy or sell positions in forward contracts. If a seller was interested in creating a forward contract to price the future delivery of grain but lacked a commercial buyer, a speculator might sign the buyer side of the contract with the objective of finding a commercial buyer at a later date. The speculator would profit from selling the forward contract at a higher price at a later date.

Assume that a speculator took the buy side of a wheat producer's forward contract. Shortly after the wheat was contracted, prices of forward contracts began to rise. The speculator realizes that he can now sell his forward contract at a higher price—say 10 cents higher than the one he originally signed. He may then sell the contract to a commercial grain buyer for a profit, if one could be found to take the buy side. In that case, the grain buyer must be willing to accept the specific details of the original contract. The 10-cent difference between the original contract price and the resale price of the contract is worth 10 cents per bushel or $1,000 on the 10,000-bushel contract.

The wheat producer could also transfer title, perhaps to a speculator or another commercial producer of wheat. He thereby avoids delivering his wheat at lower prices and eliminates the danger of having to make good on a yield loss due to bad weather or pests. Again, the wheat producer's ability to offset his original contractual commitment was dependent upon the willingness of another individual to accept the predetermined contract specification. Unlike the speculator who assumed the buy side of the contract and made a profit, the wheat producer must pay the individual taking over his contractual commitment the difference between the original price and the current market price. Remember, the producer's forward contract was priced prior to a price rise.

As you can see, trading or speculating in grain by forward contracts is cumbersome, inefficient, and restrictive to active involvement. To encourage smooth transfer of forward contracts between interested parties, midwestern grain dealers established the Chicago Board of Trade in 1848. The existence of a centralized marketplace pointed up the need for streamlined contracting procedures. Over time, these forward contracts acquired certain standards as to quantity, quality, commodity, delivery place, and delivery date. They thus became similar to modern futures contracts, one of the most flexible, innovative pricing mechanisms in the history of commerce.

As forward contracts became more standardized, speculators assumed a pivotal role in commodity market pricing. Standardization gave all participants in the commodity markets a greater opportunity to initiate and offset buy or sell positions in contracts for delivery of commodities at a set date and place in the future.

Futures Contracts

Like forward contracts, futures contracts had only one buyer and one seller at any moment in time. The creation of a contract simply depended on one buyer and one seller agreeing on a price. All other specifications were standardized.

To offset a contractual commitment in the futures market, a buyer or seller needed only to find a substitute seller or buyer. Thus, initiating and offsetting were carried out in the same way. If an individual wanted to assume the buy side of a contract, he would simply offer to buy from someone who was willing to sell. To offset the position, the contract buyer would then sell the contract to a third party, and the new buyer would assume responsibility for the terms of the contract.

Because futures contracts are standardized, ownership, transfer, and substitutions are done without endangering the original purpose of the forward market: to set price and facilitate delivery. Futures contracts could change hands many times. A seller might enter the futures market by selling a futures contract to a buyer who was a speculator. The buy side of the seller's contract could be traded numerous times before actual delivery was made. Historically, the increased use of futures by the speculator made the market more efficient and actually subdued the price fluctuation.

Without active involvement of the speculator, buyer and seller price spreads can widen and prices can shift dramatically. Furthermore, without speculative activity in commodity futures, the consumer would have to pay higher food prices to compensate grain dealers for violent price swings due to temporary gluts and shortages of commodities. The use of futures by commercials and the activity of speculators willing to buy and sell broadened the alternatives available to commodity producers and processors while reducing costs for the end user.

2

HEDGING IN THE FUTURES MARKETS

Hedging—Key to Risk Transference

Hedging is the activity by which producers and users of commodities lock in the price of future delivery. Commercial firms take advantage of futures contracts hedging.

Without hedgers, commodity futures exchanges would be no more than gambling casinos, creating instead of deferring risk. Hedging allows commercial interests to transfer risk. Hedging also links futures prices to cash prices and imposes a natural discipline on the markets because the possibility of delivery hangs over each transaction. Rarely, however—only about 3 percent of the time—do futures transactions result in delivery. Unlike forward contracts, futures are not an arena for the actual delivery of cash commodities.

There are two types of hedges that can be used in the futures market—the short hedge and the long hedge. The terms *short* and *long* refer to the position the hedger assumes in the futures market. A hedger who is interested in the sell side of the futures contract will establish a short hedge; short is this industry's term for sell. The long hedger will establish a position in the buy side of the futures contract.

The Short Hedge for Commodity Sellers

An individual or corporation enters into a short hedge to establish the price of a commodity that is to be delivered in the future. If you assume the sell side of a futures contract, then you are short the commodity. Remember, of course, that a commodity can be sold before making the actual delivery. A producer could sell a commodity months before the delivery date—even before the crop is planted—to secure the price of a sale to be made at some future date. Through futures he can both time and price his sales without locking in a pricing decision. He has the flexibility to offset his decision, to take his losses or profits and reprice later, or to hold the hedge until the delivery date of the futures contract.

Futures sales are often a temporary measure for producers, used to cover the time period prior to selling crops in the cash market.

The Short Hedge during Falling Prices

Imagine a wheat farmer who hedges by selling a futures contract two months before he expects to harvest the wheat. At harvest time he may decide to deliver the crop to a local cash market buyer. He would then offset his futures commitment before making delivery to the cash buyer. If the wheat prices fall, the value of the cash commodity declines. The producer will lose on the cash wheat he owns, but he will profit on the futures market short position. Normally, these futures profits roughly—sometimes exactly—offset the cash losses.

By hedging, the producer protects himself against the risk of price decline. He rightly assumes that futures prices will fluctuate in tandem with cash market prices. If cash prices rise, futures market prices should rise. If futures prices fall, cash markets should likewise fall. That is why hedging is uniquely suited to the businessperson who views his or her function as a risk manager.

Profits on cash transactions offset losses in futures and vice versa. The offsetting profits and losses inherent in hedging allow the price to be fixed prior to the final cash transaction.

The Short Hedge during Rising Prices

Short hedging, of course, cuts both ways. It protects against losses on inventory but also deprives the hedger of windfall profits should prices rise.

If prices rise, a short hedger will incur a loss in the futures market but the increased value of the grain inventory will compensate for it. He would have had more money in his pocket had he not hedged, but he was willing to forego windfall gains to protect against a selling price that could eliminate all profit.

When asked for the key to his success, one of the greatest traders of all time once remarked, "I always sell too soon." As for traders, so also for competent hedgers—calculated risk, not greed, produces a successful hedging program. Many hedgers sell when the bottom line profit, not the price, looks good.

The following example will reinforce your understanding of the hedge concept.

Short Hedge Mathematics

A cattle producer notices that the price of cattle on, say, June 10 is profitable to his operation, but his cattle will not be ready for market until October 1. He usually markets his fattened cattle in Guymon, Oklahoma, where on June 10 the price is $67.00 per hundred pounds (CWT). On the same date, the price for the October live cattle contract is $68.50 CWT. Since his cattle are not ready for market, he cannot take advantage of the profitable price in Guymon but he could assume the sell side of the October futures contract. As long as October futures prices rise and fall with the cash Guymon price, the cattle producer will be protected by this hedge.

Date	Cash Price	Futures Price
June 10	$67.00	$68.50

Suppose that from June 10 to October 1 the price of cattle falls to $60.00 CWT in Guymon, while the price of the futures contract falls to $61.50.

Date	Cash Price	Futures Price
June 10	$67.00	$68.50
Oct. 1	60.00	61.50
	$ 7.00 loss	$ 7.00 profit

The cattle producer would have to deliver cattle at the reduced value of $60.00 CWT in Guymon, but the futures market transaction would provide a $7.00 CWT profit. When the cattle producer entered the futures market as a seller at $68.50, the buyer of the contract obligated himself to pay that price for the future delivery of cattle. When prices fell, the buyer was obligated to pay the difference between the current price and the price at the time of entering the contract. Thus, even though the price fell, the cattle producer was able to receive $60.00 CWT for the cattle he delivered to Guymon plus $7.00 CWT profit from the futures transaction for a total of $67.00 CWT—the price he originally felt was profitable.

In this example, the cattleman chose not to deliver through the futures market. Instead, he delivered to the convenient local cash market and used the futures market to lock in the favorable price. On October 1, he delivered the cattle to Guymon and offset his futures transaction by entering a buy order. Since the buy order and the original sell order were the same in every detail except price, they offset each other and left the profit of $7.00 to apply to the cash market price.

The Long Hedge for Commodity Purchasers

Individuals or corporations needing to buy commodities can hedge
the risk of a price increase by assuming a buy hedge in the futures
market. A buy hedge, frequently called a long hedge, will protect the
user of a commodity from the increased price of a commodity to be
purchased in the future. An easy way to remember the meaning of
the term long is to think of the word *belong*. If you buy something,
then it belongs to you. Therefore, you are long if you buy.

A long hedge will result in futures profits as the price increases in
the cash markets. As cash prices rise, the user pays more for his
inputs but his futures profits could offset that higher price. He
thereby ends up paying a lower net price. He simply deducts the
futures profits from the higher price.

Many long hedgers let a cost formula guide their decisions. They
calculate their breakeven and determine at what price the input
materials produce a desired profit. Suppose at some point in time
commodity prices offer attractive profits but the user lacks storage
or capital to purchase the commodity. He may choose to hedge that
future purchase in the futures market and thereby secure the lower
price. Consider the following example of the long hedge.

Suppose that a manufacturer of copper wire wound electric
motors uses 100,000 pounds of copper per month. Due to the
considerable cost of inventorying the copper and the expense of
tying up large amounts of capital, the motor manufacturer is in the
practice of buying copper on a monthly basis. The inventory manufacturer in cooperation with other decision makers in the motor
company soon became aware that their pricing of electric motors is
profitable if copper remains in a range of 75-80 cents per pound. If
prices rise above 85 cents per pound, profit diminishes to no more
than breakeven before the manufacturer has a chance to raise its
electric motor prices.

On January 6, the price of copper in the cash market is 77 cents.
The July copper futures market is trading at 80 cents on January 6.
The motor manufacturer has just purchased 100,000 pounds of
copper that will last until the first part of February. Fearful that the
price of cash copper will rise above 80 cents and perhaps much
higher, the inventory manager considers establishing a long hedge
for the copper the company will need between early February and
July. The inventory manager will buy 100,000 pounds of copper on
the following dates:

February 6	100,000
March 6	100,000
April 6	100,000
May 6	100,000
June 6	100,000

That's 500,000 pounds of copper or 20 copper futures contracts, each representing 25,000 pounds. The inventory manager decides to hedge his copper purchases for the next five months by taking a long position of 20 contracts in the July copper contract. As he is making the monthly purchases, he intends to offset the corresponding number of contracts. On January 6, the inventory manager entered the copper futures market by buying 20 contracts at 80 cents.

Date	Cash Price	Futures Price
Jan 6	77 cents per lb.	Buy 20 contracts of July copper futures contracts at 80.00 cents

The following table represents the cash market purchase of the inventory manager and the price at which he offsets his copper futures positions.

Date	Cash Price	Futures Price
Feb 6	Buy 100,000 lbs at 78.50 cents	Sell to offset 4 contracts of July copper at 82.00 cents
Mar 6	Buy 100,000 lbs at 78.00 cents	Sell to offset 4 contracts of July copper at 81.00 cents
Apr 6	Buy 100,000 lbs at 80.00 cents	Sell to offset 4 contracts of July copper at 83.50 cents
May 6	Buy 100,000 lbs at 82.00 cents	Sell to offset 4 contracts of July copper at 85.00 cents
June 6	Buy 100,000 lbs at 85.00 cents	Sell to offset 4 contracts of July copper at 85.50 cents

Note that the copper price did increase as the motor manufacturer feared, even to the level that would put him on the brink of losing money on the sale of electric motors. Let's examine the success of this long hedge on a monthly basis.

On February 6, he offset four contracts of copper at 82 cents. Since he bought them at 80 cents, that's a 2-cent profit that can be used to reduce the cash purchase price from 78.50 to 76.50—a net price that is less than the January 6 cash purchase of copper.

Date	Cash Price	Futures Price	
Jan 6		Long at	80.00 cents
Feb 6	Buy at 78.50 cents	Short to offset at	82.00 cents
		Profit	2.00 cents

Net February 6 purchase price as a result of the hedge: 76.50 cents.

The following diagrams show the net purchase price of copper for each of the months that the copper buyer hedged.

Date	Cash Price	Futures Price	
Jan 6		Long at	80.00 cents
Mar 6	Buy at 78.00 cents	Short to offset at	81.00 cents
		Profit	1.00 cents

Net March 6 purchase price as a result of the hedge: 77.00 cents.

Date	Cash Price	Futures Price	
Jan 6		Long at	80.00 cents
Apr 6	Buy at 80.00 cents	Short to offset at	83.50 cents
		Profit	3.50 cents

Net April 6 purchase price as a result of the hedge: 76.50 cents.

Date	Cash Price	Futures Price	
Jan 6		Long at	80.00 cents
May 6	Buy at 82.00 cents	Short to offset at	85.00 cents
		Profit	5.00 cents

Net May 6 purchase price as a result of the hedge: 77.00 cents.

Date	Cash Price	Futures Price	
Jan 6		Long at	80.00 cents
June 6	Buy at 85.00 cents	Short to offset at	85.50 cents
		Profit	5.50 cents

Net June 6 purchase price as a result of the hedge: 79.50 cents.

The average of the net purchase prices for copper as a result of the hedge is 77.30 cents—only 3/10 of a cent more than the purchase made January 6. Notice that the price rose dramatically during the time period. The average cash price was 80.70 cents. The difference of 3.40 cents between the result of the hedge and the average cash prices on the purchase of 500,000 pounds saved the motor manufacturer $17,000 while not increasing the amount of the company's typical copper inventory.

$$3.40 \times 500,000 \text{ pounds copper} = \$17,000$$

The Combination of Long and Short Hedges

Under certain circumstances, futures can permit a business to hedge both input costs and output prices.

For example, a livestock producer might price cattle or hogs in the futures market and feed costs in the corn, wheat, and soybean meal markets. Now that costs and market prices are known, the producer can concentrate on what he or she does best—raising meat efficiently.

Grain producers have fewer options to choose from, but with the advent of energy and financial futures, large-scale operators can stabilize up to 50 percent of their costs. Grain exporters efficiently use this complete hedge concept and price not only the cost of the grain they sell, but also the currency rates involved in international sales as well as the variable rates on inventory financing through the T-bill and CD futures.

Considerations in Hedging

Once a hedger has locked in a particular price for the purchase or sale of a commodity, there are two major considerations that can change the effect of the hedge. If the hedger does not take into consideration the cost of holding a commodity in inventory, these carrying charges can add risks. If the value of the hedged commodity in the cash market does not parallel the futures price action, an additional risk develops.

The Impact of Carrying Charges

Carrying charges are a critical consideration for anyone holding a commodity in inventory. Carrying charges are the cost of carrying or holding a commodity in inventory. These costs include insurance; the storage facility; spoilage, deterioration, or shrinkage; and the interest on the money represented in the value of the inventory.

By far, the highest cost component of the carrying charge is the interest rate—particularly when rates are above 10 percent. Interest rates can be the swing factor in a profitable crop or a foreign grain sale. Seasoned hedgers watch the cost of carrying and financing their inventory like a hawk. Short hedgers must take the cost of carrying charges into consideration prior to establishing a hedge; they want the futures market to compensate them for carrying charges.

Futures can compensate for carrying the commodity, but they don't always do so. In most markets, when futures offer carrying charges to short hedgers the price of each successive futures month is higher than the one nearer term. For example, March is higher than December, and May is above March. These price increments tell market participants to buy, store, and sell later at a profit. These returns should net out to about zero after deducting the cost of carrying the commodity between now and the time of future delivery.

In a carrying charge market, futures prices may stairstep to higher prices as follows:

Cash price: $3.10   (Current price)
Nearby futures price: $3.20   (December)
Deferred futures price: $3.40   (March)
Next deferred futures price: $3.60   (May)

The price difference between the nearby and deferred or later months is the carrying charge.

Carrying charges may or may not exist in the futures market, and they probably won't exist in a bull market in most commodities. Also, it is unlikely that the market would ever exhibit a full carrying charge. Futures rarely compensate investors for the full cost of keeping a commodity in storage for the designated time.

Understanding the Basis

Only about 3 percent of all futures contracts result in delivery of the cash commodity through the facilities offered by the commodity futures exchanges. In most instances, hedgers take advantage of a futures price to lock in a price while they prepare to make or take delivery of the commodity in the cash market.

By assuming a futures position as a hedge for days, weeks, or even months, hedgers can insulate their business from adverse price increase or decline. Most hedgers opt for their local cash market to acquire the cash commodity. Timing the unwinding and placing of a hedge demands that the hedger monitor seasonal fluctuations between their local cash price and the futures price.

Basis is defined as the local cash market price minus the futures price. Since the cash price is normally somewhat less than the futures price, the basis is typically a negative number (some increment less than futures).

Basis can and often does fluctuate, just like actual prices. For most markets, however, the basis rise or fall is modest compared to commodity price swings. When the basis changes, hedgers should ask why. Rising and falling basis may give the hedger information on price-making factors that are independently affecting either the cash or the futures markets.

Experienced hedgers build a history for their local basis and observe changes from season to season. For example, a wide basis or a cash price much less than the futures price is common during the heavy flow of grain at harvest. Even with adequate storage, some producers may want to sell immediately upon harvest.

Buyers of grain may find that they don't have to bid the price up to get all the grain they want. Later in the year, buyers in the cash markets may cause cash prices to rise as they attempt to lure grain into the cash market.

3

THE DEVELOPMENT OF COMMODITY EXCHANGES AND THE CLEARINGHOUSE

Functions of a Commodity Exchange

The first U.S. futures exchange was developed in 1848, and today there are 12 organized commodity futures exchanges in the United States. Although today's exchanges are far more complex than their nineteenth century predecessors, their primary function remains the same—to provide the arena within which commodity futures prices are determined and to communicate those prices to the world.

The prices agreed upon at the commodity exchanges affect many people besides the brokers in the trading pit. As buyers and sellers hammer out a commodity's price, other individuals far removed from the exchange floor yet involved in the purchase and sale of that commodity rely upon the futures price to determine the market values. Only some of these traders actually price their product through brokers on the exchange floor. The rest make local cash markets but wait for the opening of futures trading to set prices.

The second function of the exchange, to communicate a price, is of paramount importance. Prices need to be disseminated swiftly and efficiently to the world. Very early in the development of commodity exchanges, telegraph wires were used to transmit futures prices. As communications systems improved, the commodity futures exchanges broadened their impact on other local exchanges. Today, communication satellites form a worldwide network that broadcasts prices around the globe. Commodity traders in Hong Kong can have access to a price determined by trading in Chicago within seconds after the actual transactions.

Even with these advanced forms of communication, the activity of determining price has not changed appreciably during the past 150 years. Futures markets resemble an auction with many auctioneers, and orders are still made by open outcry within the trading pits, or rings, at the exchanges.

Clearinghouse Functions

Similarly, the responsibilities of the clearinghouse are virtually un-changed: It provides the bookkeeping mechanism for the exchanges, and it ensures that each trade has cleared with a proper buyer and seller.

Trade Matching

Each commodity exchange has a clearinghouse through which all trades must be cleared. At the end of each trading day, the orders that contain the confirmation of a purchase or sell transaction pour into a computer. The computer matches the buyer with the seller to insure that they are in agreement as to the price of the transaction, the quantity, and the delivery month.

Few transaction errors arise because each futures contract is standardized in all factors except price. If an error is discovered by the computer, the trade is indicated by an out trade. The floor traders involved must be notified and an agreement between them determined. There must be only one buyer and one seller of each futures contract. All trades must match perfectly. Out trades, in fact, rarely occur and are promptly resolved.

Bookkeeping

This matching process, or clearing, enables the commodity fu-tures market to be a zero sum process of exchange. A buyer at a particular price is matched with a seller at that exact price. If the prices have risen since the transaction, the buyer would profit and the seller would lose in the futures market. The clearinghouse performs the bookkeeping process that enables the buyer to be credited with the profits and the seller debited for the losses of the price increase. If prices decline, the buyer is debited and the seller incurs a profit. In this manner, funds flow from one account to another, even though the account's positions have not been liquidated.

The Function of Delivery

Although only about 3 percent of the commodity contracts traded are actually delivered, the threat of delivery causes a close relationship between cash and futures. For example, if the futures price moves too far out of line from the cash price, professional traders will try to realign them by selling the high priced and buying the low priced market. Successful hedging demands that cash prices and futures prices track a parallel course, as indicated in Chapter 2. More importantly, as a commodity goes into the delivery period, the cash price and futures price should converge.

Prices naturally converge as the futures delivery month approaches. If the cash price trades too high relative to the futures price, traders will exploit this aberration by selling cash and buying futures. If the cash price trades too low relative to futures, traders will buy the cash then sell futures and deliver the cash commodity to futures. In reality, commodity traders understand this phenomenon, so it rarely occurs.

Without the guarantee of delivery the commodity market would have little integrity. The clearinghouse ensures that, when necessary, delivery will result from a contractual position. Regulations regarding delivery are discussed in Chapter 6.

Volume and Open Interest Reports

Volume and open interest figures benchmark the degree of activity and amount of participation of traders in the individual futures markets. Volume is the velocity of trading and open interest measures the number of contracts held at the conclusion of a trading session.

Volume reported daily by the commodity clearinghouses indicates the number of contracts traded during that day. Remember, this is the *number of contracts* traded during the day, not the sum of the buyers and sellers. For every contract traded, there is one buyer and one seller. To determine the volume of trading, simply count either all of the buyers or all of the sellers. The number of contracts traded includes the creation of new contracts, the transfer of either the buy side or the sell side of a contract, or the elimination of a contract. The example below shows how volume figures are calculated.

Trader A establishes a short position; Trader B establishes a long position.

Contract Created

A	B
Short	Long
Seller	Buyer

Trader B effects a long position by selling; Trader C buys, thereby accepting the opposite side of the contract with Trader A.

Transfer of Long Position

A	B	C
Short	Offset	Long
Seller	Seller	Buyer

Trader C offsets by selling; Trader A offsets by buying.

Contract Eliminated

A	C
Offset	Offset
Buyer	Seller

If the above transactions were the only ones to occur during a trading day, the total volume would be three contracts:

- Traders A and B initiated a contract.
- Traders B and C transferred the buy side of a contract.
- Traders C and A eliminated the contract.

These three types of transactions, repeated thousands of times each day on an active commodity exchange, constitute the day's volume.

Open interest is a measure of the number of contracts outstanding at the completion of the trading day. Many transactions may occur in a given day without initiating any new contracts or eliminating existing contracts; futures contracts may merely change hands. After the dust has cleared, open interest will indicate the number of contracts that are held by participants in the market. To understand open interest, follow the example below:

Day 1:   Trader A buys.
Trader B sells.
Trader C buys.
Trader D sells.

If these were the only transactions on the first day, the open interest would be two contracts.

Day 2:   Trader E buys.
Trader A sells.

If these were the only transactions taking place on the second day, the open interest would still be two contracts. Trader A simply transferred his position to Trader E.

Day 3:   Trader F buys.
Trader G sells.

> Trader B buys to offset.
> Trader C sells to offset.
> Trader E sells to offset.
> Trader D buys to offset.

At the end of the third day only one contract survives, so the open interest is one.

To test your knowledge of volume, go back and determine the volume for each of the three days.

Day 1: The volume was two. Two contracts were initiated.
Day 2: The volume was one. One contract was transferred.
Day 3: The volume was three. Two contracts were offset and one contract was initiated.

This example shows that a day of high volume can actually have a relatively small impact on open interest; i.e., if the volume was heavily represented by contract transferrals and the same number of contracts were initiated as were eliminated, open interest would remain static.

Volume figures are important in determining the liquidity of the market—the characteristic that allows orders to be filled without producing a dramatic effect on the price of the commodity. If there is low volume during a day's trading in a particular commodity, liquidity may suffer. Low volume indicates that few people are trading a commodity at that particular time and price.

Open interest, as the name implies, indicates the growing or declining interest in a commodity as reflected by the number of participants holding, initiating, or liquidating positions.

Daily Price Limits

Occasionally, newspaper or magazine articles report the commodities markets being *locked up the limit* or *locked down the limit*. These terms refer to one of the price-tempering controls the commodity exchanges place on the futures markets. Trading limits, like margins, are a management technique used by the exchanges to protect the integrity of the markets. The daily price limits control the extreme price movements of the commodity futures markets; they help cool the market down as prices move through substantial changes. The commodity exchange sets the limit, and during any day's trading price cannot move above or below the limit measured from the previous day's settlement price. Trading may continue at the price limit but may not move outside the limit up or limit down prices.

Price limits prevent futures markets from moving so much in a single day that bankruptcies and defaults result. At extremes, such as $50 silver in 1980, this danger surfaces even with limits. Despite some periods of violent price adjustments over the last century, never has an exchange failed to meet its financial obligations. Few other markets can boast of such integrity and efficiency.

Because the markets must trade within a limited price span, participants are assured that they cannot profit or lose beyond that limit in one day's trading. Of course, the market can move the price limit for several days and make it difficult for individuals with a losing position to exit the market. This eventuality is a risk inherent in commodity trading. Limits give a brokerage house time to notify a customer to supply additional funds.

Understanding the Clearinghouse by Following a Trade

Suppose that a commodity trader analyzes the factors affecting the price of wheat and determines that the price will rise. He feels he can make a speculative profit by assuming a long position in the futures markets. After examining relevant factors such as the margin requirement, minimum price fluctuation, various delivery months, and recent price activity, he decides that $4.70 would be a good price at which to buy. He has fulfilled the requirements for establishing a commodity trading account (as discussed in Chapter 8) and has adequate funds in his account to assume a position in the wheat market. When the trader is ready to speculate in wheat, he calls his broker—a registered AP (Associated Person)—and places an order. The AP writes down the order information and repeats it back to the customer: "Buy 5,000 bushels March wheat at $4.70." The AP will time-stamp the order at the moment he or she receives it from the customer and transmit it to the order taker at the trading desk on the floor of the exchange. The manner of communicating the order is determined by the AP or the brokerage. A wire service may be used to transmit a copy of the order to the exchange floor, or a telephone may be used to transmit the order to the order desk.

An order received at the order desk is immediately time-stamped and given to a runner on the floor of the exchange. The runner carries the order from the desk to a floor broker in the trading pit. (Some brokers serve a single brokerage house, while others may trade for several.) The floor broker then attempts to fill the order by open outcry. The combination of hand signals and open outcry enables the broker to determine if anyone else in the trading pit would like to sell 5,000 bushels of March wheat for $4.70. If he finds a seller, a transaction is made.

Both the buyer and the seller (floor brokers) indicate on their respective orders the price of the transaction, the name code of the individual with whom the transaction was made (each floor broker wears a badge with a two- or three-letter code as identification), the time bracket of the transaction, and other pertinent information as described in Chapter 6. The filled order is then given to a runner who returns it to the order desk. There it is again time-stamped and the confirmation of the transaction is communicated back to the AP either by phone or telex. The AP then notifies the customer of the transaction. Transactions like this are made thousands of times during the trading day at commodity exchanges around the country.

Types of Traders

There are two basic types of commodity traders—hedgers and speculators—and within each of these broad categories there are further designations.

The Position Trader

Position traders generally hold a position in the market for more than a single day. Their objective is to obtain profit by holding a position in the market for two days, a week, a month, or more.

The Day Trader

Day traders try to make a profit in a brief time span—less than one day. They will enter the market perhaps several times during the trading day but will always be out of the market by the time it closes. A market usually has at least a modest trading range during the day. The range is the span from the lowest price to the highest price for the day. Day traders try to take advantage of that range while avoiding the higher commissions that are paid when a position is held overnight.

The Scalper

Scalpers are pit traders who seek extremely short-term positions in the market. Their strategy is to take small but numerous profits as prices fluctuate during the day. In a futures market, scalpers play a role similar to specialists in the stock market. As orders flow into the trading pit, scalpers buy or sell the order for a brief moment, hoping to resell or rebuy at a profit. They act as market makers but are not assigned that role by the exchange. Their voluntary status sets them apart from stock specialists who are assigned by the exchange to accept all stock trades that are brought to them if the orders are acceptable pursuant to the price of the stock at that moment. Scalpers are not required to accept such orders but may do so voluntarily.

The Spreader

Spreaders try to make a profit by taking a long (or short) position in one commodity month or market and a short (or long) position in another commodity month or market. They trade the price change difference between the two positions in hopes of a profit. A spreader might, for instance, buy a nearby contract and sell a distant one, expecting that the rise and resulting profit in the nearby contract would be greater than the rise and resulting loss in the distant one.

The different types of spreads can be described by market (exchange), commodity, and delivery month. A spread that is long July Chicago Board of Trade corn and short September Chicago Board of Trade corn would be an intracommodity, interdelivery, and intramarket spread (*inter* meaning between two different entities and *intra* meaning within the same.) The spread is within the same commodity—corn; between two different delivery months—July and September; and within the same market—The Chicago Board of Trade. An example of an intercommodity spread would be one that is long corn/short wheat. An intermarket intradelivery spread would be long July Chicago Board of Trade wheat and short July Minneapolis Board of Trade wheat.

Spreads can also be described as bull or bear spreads. A bull spread is long the nearby delivery month and short a more distant delivery month. The expectation of the bull spreader is that if the price of the commodity rises the effect will be strongest in the closest delivery month. The bear spreader has the opposite opinion—that if prices are destined to decline, the nearby month will be affected more severely.

Also popular are the crush spread and new crop/old crop spread. The former is executed within the soybean complex by spreading soybeans against their products, soybean meal and soybean oil. The term *crush* is derived from the ancient process of crushing soybeans under high pressure to extract the oil. Since the soybean processor purchases soybeans and sells their oil and meal, a crush spread would be long soybean and short soybean oil and meal. A reverse crush spread would be short soybeans and long soybean oil and meal. A new crop/old crop spread may also be described as an interseason spread. This type of spread would have one leg in one of the delivery months available to market a crop that has already been harvested, and the other leg in the delivery available to price the unharvested crop. This is a popular spread when opposing factors are affecting growing crops and crops in storage.

PART TWO

MARKET ANALYSIS AND THE FUTURES MARKETS

Introduction

Before initiating a position in the futures market, one should analyze the commodity to determine its price direction. There are literally thousands of techniques used to analyze the futures market's price action, ranging from sophisticated computer systems to seat-of-the-pants type commodity price analysis. Nearly all analysis techniques fall into two major groups: fundamental analysis and technical analysis.

Part Two will explore both techniques, beginning with the discussion of fundamental analysis in this chapter.

4

THE FUNDAMENTAL APPROACH

Fundamental Analysis—The Study of Supply and Demand

Fundamental analysis concerns itself with supply and demand factors of a particular commodity. Fundamentalists believe that the relationship between supply and demand determines where prices are headed from their present position. If there is a relatively short supply of a commodity and a stable or increasing demand, one would expect prices to rise. On the other hand, if there is an abundant supply and a diminishing demand, prices should fall.

The most common tool of the fundamental analyst is the fundamental model—a compilation of supply and demand information that includes some method of relating historical supply and demand factors to past and current prices. Before building a fundamental model, one must understand these economic factors.

Supply and Demand Factors

Supply includes production plus existing inventory. For example, the supply of grain includes grain harvested plus grain not yet consumed from prior harvests. Similarly, the supply of gold includes new gold extracted from mining ore; salvage from scrap or meltdown of artifacts; and bullion and coins held by investors, bankers, and government treasuries. Grain is a pure commodity that is perishable and produced for consumption. Gold, at the other extreme, is a quasi-commodity available in vast quantities through decades of hoarding due to its history as a storehouse for value.

Fundamental analysts refer to inventory left over from previous harvests or marketing years as *carryover* or *carryout*. They view the carryout as stocks carried over from previous years' harvests into the new marketing year. As is evident in the case of gold versus grain, the definition of supply must be modified depending on the commodity's characteristics.

The factors associated with demand include usage and export of the commodity; the amount of the commodity consumed or converted into finished products; and depletion of the commodity through spoilage, waste, or unaccounted disappearance.

After identifying supply and demand factors, the fundamentalist uses them to evaluate current supply and demand characteristics in relation to ones from previous years. Constructing a table or mathematical formula for these factors, the fundamentalist will then assess the price level historically represented by supply and demand levels.

Following are sample supply and demand tables for some commodities traded in futures markets:

Commodity: U.S. Cotton	1979/80	1980/81
Area	Million Acres	
Planted	14.0	14.5
Harvested	12.8	13.2
	Pounds	
Yield per harvested acre	547	404
	Million 480-lb. bales	
Beginning stocks	4.0	3.0
Production	14.6	11.1
Supply, total	18.6	14.2
Mill use	6.5	5.9
Exports	9.2	5.9
Use, total	15.7	11.9
Ending stocks/carryout	3.0	2.7

Source: The United States Department of Agriculture.

Commodity: Corn	1979/80	1980/81
Area	Million Acres	
Planted	81.4	84.0
Harvested	72.4	73.0
	Bushels	
Yield per harvested acre	109.7	91.0
	Million Bushels	
Beginning stocks	1,304	1,617
Production	7,939	6,645
Imports	1	1
Supply, total	9,244	8,263
Feed and residual	4,519	4,139
Food, seed, and industrial use	675	735
Domestic, total	5,194	4,874
Exports	2,433	2,355
Use, total	7,627	7,229
Ending stocks/carryout, total	1,617	1,034
Farm-owned residence	636	185
CCC inventory	256	238
Free stocks	725	611

Source: The United States Department of Agriculture.

Commodity: U.S. Wheat	1979/80	1980/81
Area	Million Acres	
Planted	71.4	80.6
Harvested	62.5	71.0
	Bushels	
Yield per harvested acre	34.2	33.4
	Million Bushels	
Beginning stocks	924	902
Production	2,134	2,374
Imports	2	2
Supply, total	3,060	3,278
Food	596	614
Seed	101	114
Feed and residual	86	52
Domestic, total	783	780
Exports	1,375	1,510
Use, total	2,158	2,290
Ending stocks/carryout, total	902	988
Farmer-owned residence	250	360
CCC inventory	200	196
Free stocks	452	432

Source: The United States Department of Agriculture.

World Silver Supplies					
New Production	1976	1977	1978	1979	1980
Mexico	42.6	47.0	50.8	53.7	51.5
United States	34.3	38.2	39.4	38.1	31.0
Canada	41.2	42.8	40.2	36.9	33.3
Peru	35.6	36.1	37.0	42.8	40.5
Other South and Central American Countries	18.8	20.5	22.3	20.5	20.5
Total W. Hemisphere	172.5	184.6	190.7	192.0	176.8
Outside W. Hemisphere					
Australia	25.5	27.4	24.9	26.6	27.5
Other countries	49.0	55.4	52.9	51.4	50.7
Total	74.5	82.8	77.8	78.0	78.2
Total New Production	247.0	267.4	268.5	270.0	255.0
Other Supplies					
U.S. Treasury	1.3	0.4	0.1	0.1	0.1
Stocks of Foreign Governments	7.0	5.0	8.4	3.1	5.2
Demonetized Coin	55.0	23.0	14.0	25.5	55.0
India and Pakistan	70.0	40.6	45.5	33.5	41.7
Salvage and misc. sources	86.1	94.2	96.5	80.5	121.5
Liquidation of (additions to) privately held stocks	0.8	26.4	45.9	34.9	(122.6)
Total other supplies	220.2	189.6	210.4	177.6	100.9
Available for World Consumption	467.2	457.0	478.9	447.6	355.9

Source: Handy & Harman. In millions of troy ounces.

World Consumption of Silver

Arts and Industries	1976	1977	1978	1979	1980
United States	170.5	153.6	160.2	157.2	119.7
Canada	9.5	8.8	9.0	8.1	6.8
Mexico	6.5	5.5	5.8	5.5	3.5
United Kingdom	28.0	32.2	29.0	26.5	20.5
France	19.0	20.6	22.2	21.5	20.2
W. Germany	50.8	59.5	47.2	37.1	29.1
Italy	32.1	33.8	41.8	33.0	24.5
Japan	60.7	63.2	64.8	68.7	61.7
India	18.0	17.6	20.0	19.0	16.0
Belgium	15.5	16.1	16.8	16.8	15.7
Other countries	26.9	22.7	25.8	26.4	22.5
Total	437.5	433.6	442.6	419.8	340.2
Coinage					
United States	1.3	0.4	0.1	0.1	0.1
Canada	8.4	0.3	0.3	0.3	0.2
Austria	6.9	3.0	4.5	5.0	4.3
France	6.7	6.9	11.1	7.7	....
W. Germany	2.9	2.6	3.6	3.7	....
Mexico	....	4.2	6.3	5.0	5.1
Other countries	3.5	6.0	10.4	6.0	6.0
Total	29.7	23.4	36.3	27.8	15.7
Total Consumption	467.2	457.0	478.9	447.6	355.9

After constructing a supply and demand table, the fundamental-ist must try to calculate the possible effects of changes in supply and demand. Elasticity of supply and demand is an important determinant of price change.

Elasticity of Demand

An important measurement which the fundamentalists derive from testing fundamental models is the elasticity of demand at various price levels. Demand is defined as the quantity of a processed or raw material commodity that is being sought at a particular price. More strictly, it measures the percentage increase or decrease in demand with each present increase or decrease in price. It can be expected that a rise in price produces a decrease in demand.

Demand is said to be elastic if it fluctuates substantially as prices rise and fall. Beef demand is quite responsive to price changes which, in turn, affect live cattle prices. As prices rise, the demand for beef declines; as prices fall, demand increases. On the other hand, salt demonstrates inelastic demand. Unlike beef, salt represents a minute share of the consumer's dollar. Therefore, fluctuations in the price of salt have little effect on the demand for the product.

If the demand for a commodity is relatively inelastic, prices can rise and fall in wild swings as supply shrivels or expands. With an inelastic demand, extremely high prices are needed to ration supply. Prices will begin to fall as supply catches up with demand.

Elasticity of Supply

The response of supply to prices depends on the method of production for the commodity and the size of reserve or invisible stocks held in various forms. Elasticity of supply refers to the quantity of a commodity supplied to the market at a particular price. In general, elastic supply can respond with larger quantities than inelastic supply when prices rise.

In the case of agricultural commodities, it is impossible to increase the supply once the planting season has passed; if prices rise after that, a greater supply cannot be created, this is an example of a short-term inelastic supply. On the longer term (year to year), agricultural commodities have an elastic supply; if prices rise, farmers will plant more acres of the crop.

Sources and Types of Fundamental Information

Following is an abbreviated list of sources of fundamental information for many actively traded commodities. The list is not comprehensive, but it does give a good indication of the copious amount of information the fundamentalist must peruse to structure a reliable analysis.

SOURCES FOR FUNDAMENTAL INFORMATION

CATTLE
Daily Cash Market Prices—Live Animals and Steer Carcasses
Six-Market and Eleven-Market Cattle Arrivals (released each morning)
Daily Livestock Slaughter (estimated each morning)
Steer: Corn Ratio (released each Monday)
USDA Estimated Meat Production (released each Friday afternoon)
USDA Cattle-On-Feed Report (issued mid-month)
USDA Cold Storage Report (issued mid-month)
USDA Livestock & Meat Situation (published six times annually)
USDA Cattle Inventory (published each January and July)
USDA Livestock Market News (published weekly)
USDA Livestock Slaughter (published monthly)

COCOA
Weekly Ghana Main Crop Purchase Figures (released Mondays, mid-September through mid-March)

Quarterly Grindings Reports (released January, April, July, October, except monthly for Netherlands)
Gill & Duffus Market Reports (published periodically throughout the year)
USDA Foreign Agriculture Circular "Cocoa" (published periodically throughout the year)
U.N. Food and Agriculture Organization Reports (published periodically throughout the year)

COFFEE
Census Bureau Roastings & Stocks
Magazines: Coffee
World Coffee & Tea
Tea & Coffee Trade Journal

COPPER
Commodity Exchange, Inc., stocks of refined copper (released daily)
London Metal Exchange stocks of refined copper (released each Monday morning)
American Metal Market (a daily trade publication)
Metals Week (a weekly trade publication)
U.S. Bureau of Mines Industry Survey (published monthly)
U.S. Copper Association Summary of Copper Statistics in the United States (published monthly)
Copper Institute Condensed Summary of WorldwideCopper Statistics (published monthly)

CORN
Daily Cash Prices and Basis Changes
USDA Weekly Export Inspections (released each Monday afternoon)
USDA Export Sales Commitments (released each Thursday afternoon)
USDA Grain Market News (published weekly)
USDA Prospective Plantings Report (issued mid-January & mid-April)
USDA Grain Stocks in All Positions Report (issued late January, April, July, October)
USDA Crop Production Report (issued mid-month, July through January)
USDA Cattle-On-Feed Report (issued monthly)
USDA Weekly Weather and Crop Bulletin

COTTON
Spot Cotton Prices (reported daily)
New York Cotton Exchange Weekly Trade Report
Census Bureau—Ginnings (reported biweekly)
Census Bureau—Consumption, Inventories, Orders (published monthly)
USDA Prospective Plantings Report (issued mid-January and mid-April)
USDA Crop Production Report (issued mid-month, July through January)
USDA Cotton Situation (published six times annually)
USDA Weekly Weather and Crop Bulletin

CURRENCIES
Balance of Trade
Current Account Balance
Long- and Short-Term Capital Movements
Wholesale and Consumer Price Indices
Real Rate of GNP Growth
Unemployment

Interest Rates
Money Supply
Industrial Productivity
U.S. Department of Commerce
Federal Reserve Board

EGGS
Daily Cash Market Prices
USDA Weekly Egg Inventory (released each Monday afternoon)
USDA Four-State Egg-Type Hatchery Report (released each Wednesday afternoon)
USDA Retail Egg Movement (released each Thursday afternoon)
USDA Commercial Egg Movement (released each Thursday afternoon)
USDA Commercial Poultry Slaughter (released each Thursday afternoon)
USDA Eggs, Chickens & Turkeys report (released mid-month)
USDA Cold Storage Report (issued mid-month)
USDA Egg Products production (released end-month)
USDA Poultry & Egg Situation (published five times annually)
USDA Poultry Slaughter (published monthly)

FROZEN CONCENTRATE ORANGE JUICE
Florida Canners Association (weekly production & movement figures issued Thursday afternoon)
USDA Cold Storage Report (issued mid-month)
USDA Fruit Situation Report (published four times annually)
USDA Crop Production Report (released monthly, October through May)
USDA Annual Summary of the Citrus Fruit Industry

GOLD
Daily London Gold Fixings
Weekly IMM Stocks (released first Wednesday evening each month)
U.S. Treasury Auction Results
IMF Auction Results
American Metal Market (a daily trade publication)
Metals Week (a weekly trade publication)
All key prices indices and economic indicators

INTEREST RATES
Monetary Trends, Federal Reserve Bank of St. Louis, St. Louis, Missouri
National Economic Trends, Federal Reserve Bank of St Louis, Missouri
International Financial Statistics, International Monetary Fund
Federal Reserve Bulletin, Federal Reserve Bank, New York, New York
American Banker
Forbes
The Money Manager
The New York Times
The Wall Street Journal

LIVE HOGS AND PORK BELLIES
Daily Cash Market Prices—Barrows & Gilts
Six-Market and Eleven-Market Hog Arrivals (released each morning)
Daily Livestock Slaughter (estimated each morning)
Chicago Pork Belly Storage Movement (released each afternoon)
Hog: Corn Ratio (released each Monday)

LIVE HOGS AND PORK BELLIES (Continued)
Weekly Pork Belly Movement & Stocks (released each Tuesday afternoon)
USDA Estimated Meat Production (released each Friday afternoon)
USDA Sliced Bacon Production (released each Friday afternoon)
Monthly Pork Belly Stocks in CME Warehouses (released early each month)
USDA Cold Storage Report (issued mid-monthly)
USDA Hogs & Pigs Report (issued March, June, September, December)
USDA Livestock & Meat Situation (published six times annually)
USDA Livestock Market News (published weekly)
USDA Livestock Slaughter (published monthly)

PLATINUM
New York Mercantile Exchange Weekly Stocks of Refined Platinum
American Metal Market (a daily trade publication)
Metals Week (a weekly trade publication)
U.S. Bureau of Mines Industry Survey (published monthly)

PLYWOOD AND LUMBER
Census Bureau — Housing Starts & Building Permits (issued mid-month)
Census Bureau Circular —"Lumber Production & Mill Stocks" (published monthly)
Census Bureau Circular —"Softwood Plywood" (published monthly)
C.C. Crow Publications (weekly trade publications)
Random Lengths (weekly and biweekly trade publications)

SILVER
Daily Gold Prices
Commodity Exchange, Inc. Stocks of Refined Silver (released daily)
Chicago Board of Trade Stocks of Refined Silver (released daily)
London Metal Exchange Stocks of Refined Silver (released each Monday)
American Metal Market (a daily trade publication)
Metals Week (a weekly trade publication)
Chicago Board of Trade Silver Review (published weekly)
U.S. Bureau of Mines Industry Survey (published monthly)
Silver Users Association Production Statistics in the United States (published monthly)
Handy and Harman Annual Silver Review

SOYBEANS
Daily Cash Prices and Basis Changes
Trade News Service (daily trade publications)
USDA Weekly Export Inspections (released each Monday afternoon)
USDA Export Sales Commitments (released each Thursday afternoon)
Oil World (a weekly trade publication)
USDA Grain Market News (published weekly)
Census Bureau—Oilseed Crushings (released end of each month)
Census Bureau—Fats & Oils Stocks (released beginning of each month)
USDA Prospective Plantings Report (issued mid-January and mid-March)
USDA Crop Production Report (issued mid-month, July through January)
USDA Soybean Stocks in All Position Reports (issued January, April, July, September)
USDA Fats & Oils Situation (published five times annually)
USDA Weekly Weather and Crop Bulletin

SOYBEAN MEAL
Daily Cash Prices and Basis Changes
Trade News Service (daily trade publications)
USDA Export Inspections—Soybeans (released each Monday afternoon)
USDA Export Sales Commitments (released each Thursday afternoon)
Oil World (a weekly trade publication)
Census Bureau—Oilseed Crushings (released end of each month)
USDA Foreign Agriculture Circular—"Fats and Oils" (published periodically throughout the year)
USDA Fats and Oils Situation (published five times annually)

SOYBEAN OIL
Daily Cash Prices and Basis Changes
Trade News Service (daily trade publications)
USDA Export Inspections—Soybeans (released each Monday afternoon)
USDA Export Sales Commitments (released each Thursday afternoon)
Oil World (a weekly trade publication)
Census Bureau—Oilseed Crushings (released end of each month)
Census Bureau—Fats & Oil Stocks (released beginning of each month)
USDA Foreign Agriculture Circular—"Fats and Oils" (published periodically throughout the year)
USDA Fats and Oils Situation (published five times annually)

SUGAR
Sugar Tender Results (reported when sales announced)
USDA Sugar Report (published monthly)
USDA Foreign Agriculture Circular—"Sugar" (published periodically throughout the year)
UN Food and Agriculture Organization Reports (published periodically throughout the year)
Private Production and Consumption Forecasts (issued periodically). Key sources:
  F. O. Licht
  E. D. & F. Mann
  C. Czarnikow

WHEAT
Daily Cash Prices and Basis Changes
USDA Weekly Export Inspections (released each Monday afternoon)
USDA Export Sales Commitments (released each Thursday afternoon)
USDA Grain Market News (published weekly)
USDA Prospective Plantings Report (issued mid-January and mid-March)
USDA Crop Production Report (issued mid-month, May through January)
USDA Winter Wheat Seedings (issued late December)
USDA Grain Stocks in All Positions Report (issued January, April, July, October)
USDA Wheat Situation (published four times annually)
USDA Weekly Weather and Crop Bulletin

5

THE TECHNICAL APPROACH

Technical Analysis—The Study of Price Action

In contrast to the fundamental analyst, the technical analyst concentrates on historical price action to determine future price action.

The technical analyst assumes that people who have a strong opinion about a commodity price will express that opinion by putting money behind a position in the futures market. Hence, the price should represent the composite opinion of all individuals involved in trading the commodity.

The technical analyst believes that price reflects all factors, including fundamental factors. Rising prices reflect aggressive buying, and declining prices result from aggressive selling. In other words, price expresses the change in demand. Therefore, in price, the technical analyst can monitor the total sum of the multiple factors represented by demand and supply.

To quantify and measure price action, technicians resort to price studies and statistical methods. Their most rudimentary tool is the bar chart, which graphically displays price action for a given time period.

Commodity Price Charting

The bar chart plots time on the X or horizontal axis and price on the Y or vertical axis. After selecting a particular span of time—one hour, one day, one week, or one month—the technical analyst plots the high and low price for that time period and connects the two prices with a vertical line or bar as shown in Figure 5.l. This vertical line represents how high or low prices have been pushed by aggressive buying and selling.

Think of the bar chart as a tug-of-war between the buyers and sellers, each trying to pull or push the market in their direction during a trading day, week, or month. A horizontal hatchmark at the end of the time period represented by the vertical line on the chart indicates the closing price. This horizontal mark acts like the flag tied on a tug-of-war rope. At a certain time in the struggle—at

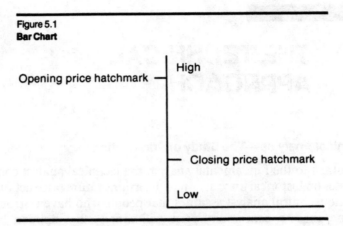

Figure 5.1
Bar Chart

Opening price hatchmark

High

Closing price hatchmark

Low

ground. On daily bar charts it represents the settlement price at the end of the trading day. On weekly charts, Friday's settlement price is usually used; on monthly charts, it is the last day of the month's settlement or closing price.

  The position of the starting or opening price for a given time

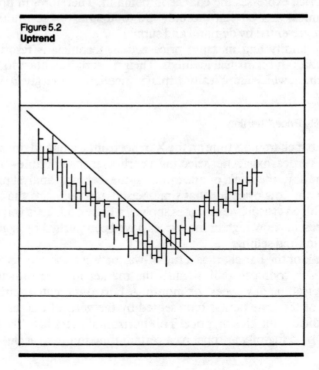

Figure 5.2
Uptrend

series can be marked with a horizontal hatchmark to the left of the vertical line. The various time periods indicated along the bar chart help the technician perceive historical price direction. Deviations from previous highs, lows, openings, and closes give an ongoing feel for the market.

Prices often move higher in a trend delineated by drawing a line connecting the reaction lows (see Figure 5.2), then move lower in a downtrend delineated by connecting the rally highs (see Figure 5.3).

When prices move higher, the technical analyst may either buy to profit from the rise in prices or sell short in the hopes that prices will fall. In either event, the decision is based strictly on price levels and technical formations.

Technical analysts look for price patterns that show a high probability for forecasting future price action. Although these patterns can improve trading odds, technical analysis is not a science and should not be used as a final authority when attempting to forecast future price movement. Just as the canvas and brush are tools to a good artist, the bar chart and other technical analysis tools are only as effective as the technician's ability to use them.

Figure 5.3
Downtrend

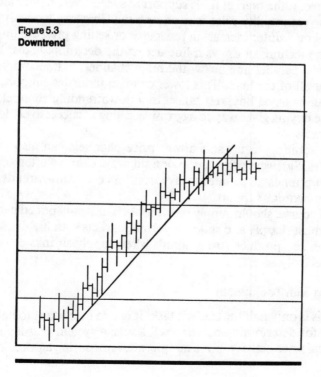

Technical formations represent market psychology as they trend higher or lower. For example, they often move in short-term uptrends and short-term downtrends, with the downtrends ending at higher levels and succeeding uptrends pushing to new highs.

Price Channels

Markets tend to move in broad channels of volatility that trend sideways, up, or down. Uptrend channels connect the successively higher lows. The top of the channel runs parallel to the lower channel line and embraces all or most rally highs for the move. As long as the trend lasts, prices should find resistance at the top of the channel band and support at the bottom. Channels help the trader forecast where prices are headed and when.

Channels measure the direction and volatility of price. Prices often trade for long periods of time within a price channel. The lower channel line indicates a point at which buying becomes more aggressive and the upper line indicates where resistance to buying occurs and selling becomes more aggressive.

Within a channel, prices trade between levels of support and resistance. If the market finds support at successively higher levels, then the commodity price is in an uptrend. Prices in a downtrend channel encounter increasing resistance or selling pressure on rallies. The technician draws a line across the declining highs, then projects a parallel line below the price channel that encompasses most or all of the lows. This lower channel indicates support, the upper downtrend line, resistance. In a downtrending channel, aggressive buying gives way to aggressive selling at successively lower price levels.

In addition to up and down, price channels can also move sideways. Sideways price action or a sideways channel often occurs when uptrends encounter heavy resistance or downtrends encounter bedrock support.

Of course, should supply conditions change, any priced pattern may adjust sharply and suddenly. Even markets with highly elastic demand can produce strong trends when supply shrinks or swells unexpectedly.

Trading with Technicals

Analysis is only half the trader's task. It is also important to have a system for determining buy and sell levels, a system that looks at historical price activity. For example, after measuring a price channel, you might gain the confidence to buy at support and sell as prices rise to resistance. Or, if you find prices moving in a sideways pattern, you might sell as they approach historical resistance areas and profit as they fall back to historical support.

This selling and buying back in a trading range works fairly well until the unexpected occurs. For example, as you trade a downtrend channel and notice that prices penetrate the downtrend line rather than reversing at resistance levels, you should rethink your strategy. If prices penetrate a downtrend line and close above that line, the market trend may have changed.

The technical trader relies on two rules of thumb regarding trendlines:

- The longer the trendline has endured, the more significant its penetration becomes.
- Penetrations of trendlines may not confirm a trend reversal, but they do confirm major highs or lows made previously and seasonal tops or bottoms.

Any trendline break is significant. If price action penetrates a trendline to the up side, then, as a technical analyst, you should at least redraw the downtrend line to include this new high, thus indicating a change in trend. Redrawing of the downtrend line becomes senseless once you perceive that a genuine uptrend is developing. Often a trendline break causes at least a temporary reversal in the market due to a loss of confidence in the prevailing trend. It shakes the confidence of those who hold short positions. Some buy back their short position and cause prices to move higher.

Head and Shoulders—The Most Reliable Technical Formation

A good analyst deciphers market psychology from price behavior at critical points in a move. One chart formation, in particular, is a good indicator of a major shift and reversal of the market's trend. Commonly called a *head and shoulders*, this formation is a favorite of many technical analysts for its reliability and profit potential.

Price activity shapes a head and shoulders top by pushing prices to a new high, not necessarily accompanied by high volume. The lower volume price rally reflects a lack of participation. Perhaps only the more astute traders or knowledgeable commercial interests took profits at these highs. After taking profits, the market-making forces allow prices to fall. From these thinly traded highs, prices often fall back to an established trendline or support area where new buying interest rallies the market once again. At this point, volume and open interest often increase. The price on this rally makes new highs for the price move.

On this rally, the rise in open interest reflects inexperienced traders entering the market. Veteran traders call this price move a weak rally, which implies that the new buyers lack financial staying power. Once the market price fails at new highs, less financially backed traders bail out. The liquidation of these long positions causes the market to drop even faster. Veteran traders use this opportunity to establish short positions on price retracements of the price drop. As less experienced traders exit long positions and veteran traders initiate short positions, the market falls rapidly. This fall in price finally discovers support as traders take profits and as new buying interest flows into the market.

This description of a head and shoulders top is actually the beginning of the end. Rallies will now fail because previous rallies already milked most of the aggressive buying out of the market. As prices fail to make new highs, confidence in a bull move wanes and the market develops into a downtrend.

Figure 5.4
Head and Shoulders Top

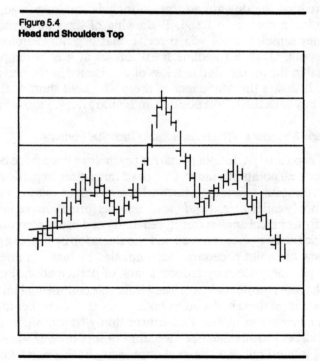

At this point, the technical analyst draws a neckline. A neckline connects areas of support which are at the vortexes or bottoms of previous rallies. This support or neckline stretches from the left shoulder under the head or price peak to the right shoulder(see Figure 5.4). The price above neckline becomes critical. For the head and shoulders to bear fruit, this neckline or support price must give way. Breaking this neckline completes the head and shoulders top and indicates a reversal of the long-term trend in prices from up to down. The technician now has a strong sell signal to position his trades.

Once this widely watched neckline gives way, the market may plunge rapidly. Low-risk sales become difficult to execute. The veteran trader keeps a watchful eye for just such a price break, waits patiently until the heaviest selling activity has run its course, then establishes short positions on a minor rally. This rise in price after breaking the neckline is known as the *pullback effect* and offers an excellent opportunity to initiate a short position. Sometimes this pullback rally runs back up to the neckline, which is now resistance above the market.

Figure 5.5
Head and Shoulders Bottom

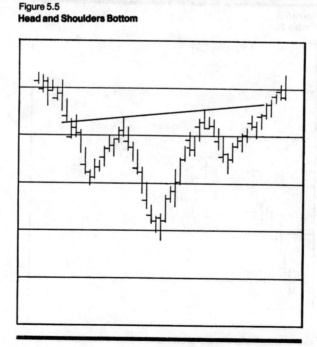

Head and shoulders formations occur at both market tops and market bottoms. When the formation occurs at a bottom it is called an inverted head and shoulders (see Figure 5.5). All the same conditions apply as with a top, but in reverse order. Knowing that head and shoulders tops and bottoms are reversal patterns can help the trader position himself for a profitable move in the opposite direction of the previous trend.

How far will prices decline from a break of the neckline? Head and shoulders formations project a price objective. To determine this objective, the technical analyst measures the vertical distance from the top of the head to the neckline. This distance is then projected down the price chart from the point at which the neckline was penetrated. If the distance from the neckline to the top of the head is 100 points, the technical analyst expects the market to move down 100 points from the breakout area.

Double and Triple Tops

Some of the strongest resistance and support areas are historical highs and historical lows, respectively. A study of historical price

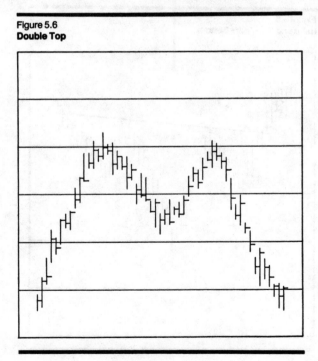

Figure 5.6
Double Top

moves will reveal many failures of price to exceed historical highs and lows. Markets will frequently stop dead on the exact price of a previous high or low before reversing to a move in the opposite direction.

Failures at major highs and lows may form double or triple tops or bottoms (see Figures 5.6 and 5.7). Traders' attitudes in the face of these failures will change from bullish to bearish, thus reducing the probability of market moves beyond those price levels. Multiple tops and bottoms offer a safe location to place a liquidating order or to protect profits, but they're not a sure thing. If market action exceeds the previous high or low, prices will probably accelerate in the direction of the current trend. If there is any doubt that a market has formed a double top or double bottom, the trader should wait for confirmation, which occurs when prices drop below the vortex of the double top or triple top.

Key Reversal Tops and Key Reversal Bottoms

A key reversal is a high probability formation. It indicates that the current market trend is likely to reverse for an undetermined

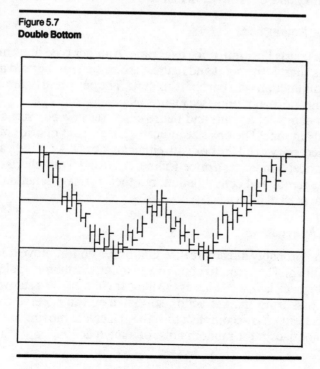

Figure 5.7
Double Bottom

period of time. The circumstances that surround a key reversal include a steep trend climaxing in a wide trading range, often at new highs, with a close near the high in the case of a top or near the low in the case of a bottom (see Figure 5.8). On the following day's trading or the key reversal day, prices move higher than the previous day's high and lower than the previous day's low, closing near the low of the day. This reversal is more definitive if accompanied by high volume, often record high volume, and new contract or all-time highs.

Island Reversal

An island reversal is similar to a key reversal but usually involves more trading days and requires a gap at either side of the island formation. Typically, the gaps are at approximately the same price level.

Continent Reversal

The continent reversal is identical to the island reversal except that it may take days or weeks to form.

Point and Figure Charts

Bar charts illustrate price over time. Another type of technical analysis chart is the point and figure chart, which can be used alone or in conjunction with bar chart analysis. The point and figure chart plots only price, not time (see Figure 5.9).

To construct a point and figure chart, select a box size and a reversal amount. The box size indicates the amount of price movement necessary to fill the box with either an X or O. An X indicates a rise in price; O indicates a price decline. Point and figure charts often indicate trends and consolidation, but their primary function is to indicate market reversals.

Moving Averages

You probably already realize that prices do not move directly up or down. They tend to chop in a sawtooth fashion from low to high, high to low, or sideways. Many traders try to remove the choppiness from market action so that they can observe overall price patterns. To accomplish this, they calculate moving averages that smooth over the random noise of market action.

Figure 5.8
Key Reversal

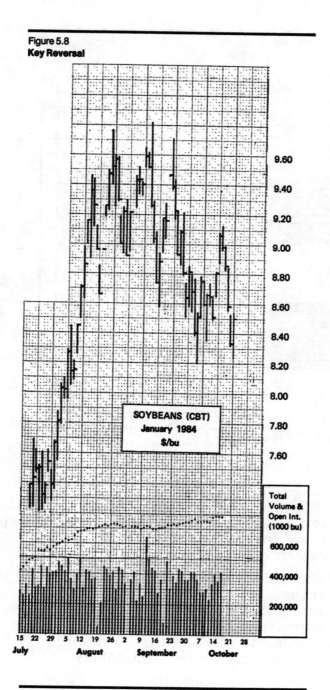

SOYBEANS (CBT)
January 1984
$/bu

9.60
9.40
9.20
9.00
8.80
8.60
8.40
8.20
8.00
7.80
7.60

Total
Volume &
Open Int.
(1000 bu)

600,000
400,000
200,000

15 22 29 5 12 19 26 2 9 16 23 30 7 14 21 28
July   August   September   October

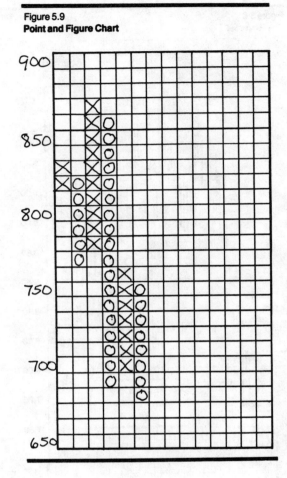

Figure 5.9
Point and Figure Chart

To calculate a moving average, total the prices for a given period of days and divide by that number of days. To calculate a 3-day moving average:

- Select the first three days' prices.
- Total them.
- Divide by 3.
- Subtract the first day and add the fourth day.
- Divide this total by 3.
- Subtract the second day and add the fifth day.

- Divide this total by 3.
- Continue as above.

Some technical analysts use moving averages simply to indicate the general trend or direction in price. Others look to them for specific buy and sell signals. To receive a sell signal, a shorter moving average must cross a longer moving average in a movement down. To receive a buy signal, the shorter average must cross the longer one in a movement higher. Figure 5.10 shows how buy and sell signals would be generated from a moving average chart.

Figure 5.10

Date	Silver $	10-Day Moving Average	20-Day Moving Average
1	8.24		
2	8.33		
3	8.29		
4	8.29		
5	8.19		
6	8.08		
7	8.1		
8	7.9		
9	7.87		
10	7.76	8.10	
11	7.91	8.07	
12	7.83	8.02	
13	7.87	7.98	
14	7.84	7.93	
15	7.84	7.9	
16	7.85	7.87	
17	7.94	7.86	
18	8.15	7.88	
19	8.2	7.91	
20	8.2	7.96	8.03
21	8.17	7.98	8.03
22	8.14	8.02	8.02
23	8.26	8.05	8.01
24	8.54	8.12	8.03
25	8.6	8.2	8.05
26	8.43	8.26	8.07
27	8.51	8.32	8.09
28	8.76	8.38	8.13
29	8.62	8.42	8.17
30	8.61	8.46	8.21
31	8.47	8.49	8.24
32	8.42	8.52	8.27
33	8.32	8.52	8.29
34	8.19	8.49	8.31
35	7.99	8.43	8.31
36	7.83	8.37	8.31
37	7.98	8.31	8.31
38	7.89	8.23	8.3

Figure 5.10 (continued)

Date	Silver $	10-Day Moving Average	20-Day Moving Average
39	7.74	8.14	8.28
40	7.89	8.07	8.26
41	7.82	8.00	8.25
42	7.66	7.93	8.22
43	7.5	7.84	8.18
44	7.3	7.76	8.12
45	7.02	7.66	8.04
46	7.16	7.59	7.98
47	7.25	7.52	7.92
48	7.16	7.45	7.84
49	6.97	7.37	7.75
50	7.2	7.30	7.68
51	7.04	7.22	7.61
52	7.1	7.17	7.55
53	7.17	7.13	7.49
54	7.03	7.11	7.43
55	7.21	7.12	7.39
56	7.18	7.13	7.36
57	7.29	7.13	7.32
58	7.09	7.12	7.28
59	7.04	7.13	7.25
60	7.09	7.12	7.21
61	7.03	7.12	7.17
62	7.15	7.12	7.14
63	7.08	7.11	7.12
64	7.17	7.13	7.12
65	7.46	7.15	7.14
66	7.61	7.2	7.16
67	7.45	7.21	7.17
68	7.54	7.26	7.19
69	7.38	7.29	7.21
70	7.44	7.33	7.22
71	7.6	7.38	7.25
72	7.55	7.42	7.27
73	7.58	7.47	7.29
74	7.15	7.47	7.3
75	7.17	7.44	7.3
76	7.19	7.4	7.3
77	7.16	7.37	7.29
78	7.25	7.34	7.3
79	7.1	7.31	7.3
80	7.15	7.29	7.31
81	7.09	7.23	7.31
82	7.01	7.18	7.3
83	6.86	7.11	7.29
84	6.89	7.08	7.28
85	6.88	7.09	7.25
86	6.87	7.02	7.21

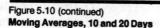

Figure 5.10 (continued)
Moving Averages, 10 and 20 Days

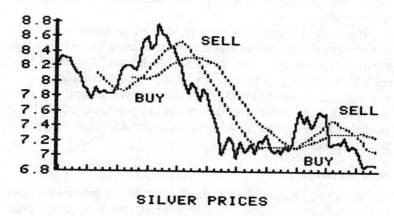

Using Averages to Explore Alternatives

I have found no holy grail for the markets, but I have developed some ways to cut down big losses and let profits run. If I want to buy a market:

- Both moving averages (10- and 20-day) must be moving higher (the 10-day above the 20-day).
- I place an order to buy in a price range between the 10-day and 20-day average.
- I place a stop below the 20-day moving average.
- I wait for prices to dip into this zone and buy only when this setback occurs.

If I want to sell a market:

- Both moving averages must be moving down (the 10-day below the 20-day).
- I place my sell order in the range between the 10-and 20-day.
- I place my stop above the 20-day moving average.
- I wait for the market price to rally into this zone. I sell short only when this occurs.

Under almost no circumstances should a position trade be

initiated when a commodity is in a trading range. It is usually best to see a clearly defined trend in which moving averages are going in the same direction and in which the long-term trend confirms short-term signals.

If a market is declining relative to the 200-day or 9.2 month moving average, the environment is bearish. Look for selling opportunities. The market is oversold when it declines substantially below the 200-day average. Start looking for buying opportunities.

The commodity group of which the market is a member should be moving in the direction of the trade. Group indexes such as those published by Wasendorf & Associates are useful for observing group price direction.

Speedline Review

Speedline analysis can effectively supplement moving average-based trading. As with most technical tools, speedline analysis can be applied to bull or bear markets. It can analyze the long-term importance of reversals and trend continuations. Developed by Edson Gould years ago, speedlines measure the speed or momentum of a trend reversal and help identify whether a reversal will unfold into a new long-term trend or is just a flash in the pan.

Bull Market Speedlines

After a period of rising, bull markets top and correct. The depth of the correction can be measured by speedlines. Figure 5.11 shows a speedline pattern for a bull market.

To measure speedlines, take the vertical distance between low A and top B and divide it into thirds. The upper speedline, drawn off the low A, cuts through the upper one-third point of the vertical line; the lower cuts through the lower one-third point of the vertical. In general, retracements in bull markets that penetrate the upper speedline, as in the chart, will sink to the lower. If the lower is penetrated by more than 2 to 3 percent, then point B may be a major top and the low at A may be penetrated.

Bear Market Speedlines

Bear market speedlines work in a reverse manner to bull market speedlines. As Figure 5.12 indicates, the vertical distance between top B and low C is divided into thirds. A bear market that penetrates the lower speedline and rallies decisively through the upper speedline is likely to reach or take out top B.

Figure 5.11
Bull Market Speedlines

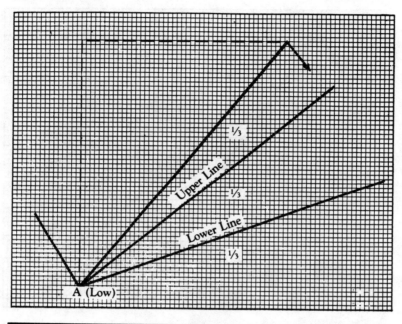

Speedlines can be watched on long-term, weekly charts to indicate reversal zones and potential tops or bottoms. They are not useful for short-term trading.

Technical Fundamentals

Technical factors refer to the patterns of price volume and open interest that suggest reversals or continuations of trends. Fundamental factors include demand and supply conditions which influence the trend in prices.

Fundamentalists and technicians normally get along with one another about as well as Republicans and Democrats. Nevertheless, technical and fundamental factors tend to blend. Take, for instance, the fundamentalist who uses basis (the price difference between the cash and futures) to view the price-making activities of a commodity market. Basis is usually expressed as a chart. Don't technical analysts use charts? Also, aren't seasonal price changes a fundamental factor and aren't they usually viewed in chart form? In reality, there

Figure 5.12
Bear Market Speedlines

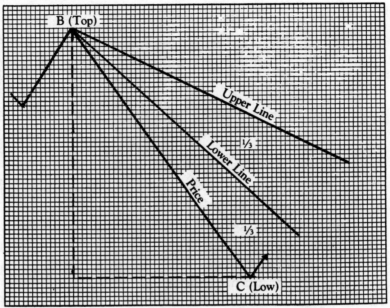

is less difference between the schools of analysis than they are willing to admit.

The difference becomes even less acute as one becomes comfortable with the technique of relative value analysis. Relative value is often best expressed in a ratio. Ratios have long been a fundamental technique—consider the hog/corn ratio, the corn/soybean ratio, the chick/feed ratio, etc. Ratios allow the trader to determine relative price and are much more valuable than spread charts.

To illustrate this, consider soybeans at $8.00 and corn at $3.50. Suppose the price of soybeans rises to $8.50 and corn to $4.00. The spread would not have changed, but the ratio would move dramatically from $2.28\frac{1}{2}$ to $2.12\frac{1}{2}$, a change of 7 percent in favor of corn. Relative value can be deceptive, though. The ratio may indicate that one commodity is gaining on another, when both commodities are actually declining in real value. This is where trend watching becomes important.

This all boils down to the fact that one should not be married to technical or fundamental analysis. Perhaps it is best to examine fundamentals in a technical way. A good trading program should include many factors and analysis techniques. Avoid putting complete faith in any one technique.

As you consider making a trade, it is best if you ask yourself the following questions:

- What is the direction of the trend on the long term? Short term?
- What are the technical factors indicating for the long term? Short term?
- Is the market gaining or losing in relative value to its sister commodities?
- What are the supply and demand characteristics for the long term? Short term?
- Are there strong seasonal and/or cyclical factors to consider?
- What is the risk-to-reward ratio?
- With the market in the present position, what is the best market entering technique?
- What signals will tell me to get out of the market?
- What money management techniques are needed for this position?

Relative Value

Relative value is an illusive concept that is difficult to trade. If I determine that the price of a particular commodity is low or oversold relative to another, I am still faced with the question of which commodity price is going to move to force the price relationship back into line.

Let us accept that the ratio of two commodity prices is actually the relative value rather than absolute spread of the prices. The relative value is determined by dividing one price into the other—relative value is a ratio of the prices. It is impossible to enter a relative value or ratioed position in the futures market, but you can enter the market in a spread. Ratios will give lead indications of entry and exit points for spreads.

The Commodities Traded as Futures Markets

Contract markets traded on designated markets are numerous and varied, but the common thread that ties them together is their economic importance as raw materials or finished products. Sometimes it is difficult to consider interest rates or stock indexes as raw materials, but these markets are as necessary as corn or pork bellies for hedging the future purchase and sale by commercial interests.

The commodity contract specifications on the following pages illustrate how a change in the value of an inventory is represented by a price change in a futures contract market.

Commodity Contract Specifications

Commodity	American Exchanges	Contract Size	Minimum Fluctuation	Daily Limit	Value of a 1¢/$1 Move
Barley	WCE	20 metric tons	10¢/ton = $2	$5 = $100	$1 = $20
Boneless beef	CME	38,000 lbs.	2.5/100¢/lb. = $9.50	1.5¢ = $570	1¢ = $380
Broilers, iced	CBOT	30,000 lbs.	2.5/100¢/lb. = $7.50	2¢ = $600	1¢ = $300
Broilers	CME	30,000 lbs.	2.5/100¢/lb. = $7.50	2¢ = $600	1¢ = $300
Butter	CME	38,000 lbs.	2.5/100¢/lb. = $9.50	1.5¢ = $570	1¢ = $380
Cattle, feeder	CME	42,000 lbs.	2.5/100¢/lb. = $10.50	1.5¢ = $360	1¢ = $420
Cattle, live	CME	40,000 lbs.	2.5/100¢/lb. = $10	1.5¢ = $600	1¢ = $400
Cocoa	CSCE	10 metric tons	$1/metric ton = $10	$88 = $880	$1 = $10
Coffee "C"	CSCE	37,500 lbs.	1/100¢/lb. = $3.75	4¢ = $1,500	1¢ = $375
Coffee "B"	CSCE	32,500 lbs.	1/100¢/lb. = $3.25	4¢ = $1,300	1¢ = $325
Commercial paper (90 day)	CBOT	$1,000,000	1 pt. = $25	50 pts. = $1,250	1 pt. = $25
Commercial paper (30 day)	CBOT	$3,000,000	1 pt. = $25	50 pts. = $1,250	1 pt. = $25
Copper	COMEX	25,000 lbs.	5/100¢/lb. = $12.50	5¢ = $1,250	1¢ = $250
Corn	CBOT	5,000 bu.	1/4¢/bu. = $12.50	10¢ = $500	1¢ = $50
Cotton no. 2	NYCE	50,000 lbs.	1/100¢/lb. = $5	2¢ = $1,000	1¢ = $500
Crude oil	NYCE	5,000 barrels	1/10¢/barrels = $5	25¢ = $1,250	1¢ = $50
Currencies:					
British pound	IMM	25,000 BP	5/100¢/BP = $12.50	5¢ = $1,250	1¢ = $250
British pound	NYFE	25,000 BP	5/100¢/BP = $12.50	None	1¢ = $250
Canadian dollar	IMM	100,000 CD	1/100¢/CD = $10	3¢ = $750	1¢ = $1,000
Canadian dollar	NYFE	100,000 CD	1/100¢/CD = $10	None	1¢ = $1,000
Dutch guilder	IMM	125,000 DG	1/100¢/DG = $12.50	1¢ = $1,250	1¢ = $1,250
French franc	IMM	250,000 FF	5/1,000¢/FF = $12.50	2¢ = $1,250	1¢ = $2,500
German deutschemark	IMM	125,000 DM	1/100¢/DM = $12.50	1¢ = $1,250	1¢ = $1,250

Commodity Contract Specifications (continued)

Commodity	American Exchanges	Contract Size	Minimum Fluctuation	Daily Limit	Value of a 1¢/$1 Move
German deutschemark	NYFE	125,000 DM	1/100¢/DM = $12.50	None	1¢ = $1,250
Japanese yen	IMM	12,500,000 JY	1/10,000¢/JY = $12.50	1/100¢ = $1,250	1¢ = $125,000
Japanese yen	NYFE	12,500,000 JY	1/10,000¢/JY = $12.50	None	1¢ = $125,000
Mexican peso	IMM	1,000,000 MP	1/1,000¢/MP = $10	1.5/100¢ = $1,500	1¢ = $10,000
Swiss franc	IMM	125,000 SF	1/100¢/SF = $12.50	1.5¢ = $1,875	1¢ = $1,250
Swiss franc	NYFE	125,000 SF	1/100¢/SF = $12.50	None	1¢ = $1,250
Eggs, fresh	CME	22,500 doz.	5/100¢/doz. = $11.25	2¢ = $450	1¢ = 225
Eggs, frozen	CME	36,000 lbs.	2.5/100¢/lb. = $9	1.5¢ = $540	1¢ = 360
Eggs, nest run	CME	22,500 doz.	5/100¢/doz. = $11.25	2¢ = $450	1¢ = 225
Flaxseed	WCE	20 metric tons	10¢/ton = $2	$10 = $200	$1 = $20
GNMA CD	CBOT	$100,000 princ	$\frac{1}{32}$ pt. = $31.25	$\frac{64}{32}$ = $2,000	1 pt. = $1,000
GNMA CDR	CBOT	$100,000 princ	$\frac{1}{32}$ pt. = $31.25	$\frac{64}{32}$ = $2,000	1 pt. = $1,000
GNMA	COMEX	$100,000 princ	$\frac{1}{64}$ pt. == $15.625	$\frac{64}{64}$ pt. = $1,000	1 pt. = $1,000
Gold	CBOT	100 oz.	10¢/oz. = $10	$50 = $5,000	1 = $100
Gold	CBOT	3 kilos	10¢/oz. = $9.60	$25 = $2,411	$1 = $96
Gold	IMM	100 troy oz.	10¢/oz. = $10	$50 = $5,000	$1 = $100
Gold	COMEX	100 troy oz.	10¢/oz. = $10	$25 = $2,500	$1 = $100
Gold, centum	WCE	100 troy oz.	10¢/oz. = $10	$35 = $3,500	$1 = $100
Hams, skinned	CME	36,000 lbs.	2.5/100¢/lb. = $9	1.5¢ = $540	1¢ = $360
Hogs, live	CME	30,000 lbs.	2.5/100¢/lb. = $7.50	1.5¢ = $450	1¢ = $300
Imported lean beef	NYME	36,000 lbs.	2/100¢/lb. = $720	1.5¢ = $540	1¢ = $360
Lumber, random length	CME	100,000 bd. ft.	10¢/1,000 bd. ft. = $10	$5 = $500	$1 = $100
Lumber, stud	CME	100,000 bd. ft.	10¢/1,000 bd. ft. = $10	$5 = $500	$1 = $100
Milo	CME	400,000 lbs.	2.5/100¢/cwt. = $10	15¢ = $600	1¢ = $40
Oats	CBOT	5,000 bu.	$\frac{1}{4}$¢/bu. = $12.50	6¢ = $300	1¢ = $50
Oats	WCE	20 metric tons	10¢/ton = $2	$5 = $100	$1 = $20
Oil, #2 heating	NYME	42,000 gal.	1/100¢/gal. = $4.20	2¢ = $840	1¢ = $420

Commodity	Exchange	Contract size			
Oil, #6 industrial fuel	NYME	42,000 gal.	1/100¢/gal. = $4.20	2¢ = $840	1¢ = $420
Orange juice	NYCE	15,000 lbs.	5/100¢/lb. = $750	5¢ = $750	1¢ = $150
Palladium	NYME	100 troy oz.	5¢/oz. = $5	$6 = $600	$1 = $100
Platinum	NYME	50 troy oz.	10¢/oz. = $5	$20 = $1,000	$1 = $50
Plywood	CBOT	76,032 sq. ft.	10¢/1,000 ft. = $7.60	$7 = $532	$1 = $76
Pork bellies	CME	38,000 lbs.	2.5/100¢/lb. = $9.50	2¢ = $760	1¢ = $380
Potatoes russet burbank	CME	80,000 lbs.	1¢/100 lbs. = $8	50¢ = $500	1¢ = $8
Potatoes	NYME	50,000 lbs.	1¢/100 lbs. = $5	50¢ = $250	1¢ = $5
Propane, liquid	NYCE	100,000 gal.	1/100¢/gal. = $10	2.5¢ = $2,500	1¢ = $1,000
Rapeseed	WCE	20 metric tons	10¢/ton = $2	$10 = $200	$1 = $20
Rye	WCE	20 metric tons	10¢/ton = $2	$5 = $100	$1 = $20
Silver	CBOT	5,000 troy oz.	1/10¢/oz. = $5	20¢ = $1,000	$1 = $50
Silver	COMEX	5,000 troy oz.	1/10¢/oz. = $5	50¢ = $2,500	$1 = $50
Silver coins, US	IMM	$5,000 (5 bags at $1,000)	$2/bag = $10	$150 = $750	$1 = $5
Silver coins, US	NYME	$1,000 (10 bags at $1,000)	$1/bag = $10	$300 = $3,000	$1 = $10
Soybeans	CBOT	5,000 bu.	¼¢/bu. = $12.50	30¢ = $1,500	1¢ = $50
Soybean meal	CBOT	100 tons	10¢/ton = $10.00	$10 = $1,000	$1 = $100
Soybean oil	CBOT	60,000 lbs.	1/100¢/lb = $6.00	1¢ = $600	1¢ = $600
Sugar no. 11	CSCE	112,000 lbs.	1/100¢/lb = $11.20	½¢ = $560	1¢ = $1,120
Sugar no. 12	CSCE	112,000 lbs.	1/100¢/lb = $11.20	½¢ = $560	1¢ = $1,120
Sunflower seeds	MGE	100,000 lbs.	1¢/100 lbs = $10.00	50¢ = $500	1¢ = $10
Treasury bills (13-week)	IMM	$1,000,000	1 pt. = $25.00	60 t. = $1,500	1 pt. = $25
Treasury bills (1-year)	IMM	$250,000	1 pt. = $25.00	50 pt. = $25	1 pt. = $25
Treasury bills (90-day)	COMEX	$1,000,000	1 pt. = $25.00	60 pt. = $1,500	1 pt. = $25
Treasury bills (91-day)	NYFE	$1,000,000	1 pt. = $25.00	100 pt. = $2,500	1 pt. = $25

Commodity Contract Specifications (*continued*)

Commodity	American Exchanges	Contract Size	Minimum Fluctuation	Daily Limit	Value of a 1¢/$1 Move
Treasury bonds	CBOT	$100,000	$\frac{1}{32}$ pt. = $31.25	$\frac{96}{32}$ pt. = $2,000	1 pt. = $1,000
Treasury bonds	NYFE	$100,000	$\frac{1}{32}$ pt. = $31.25	$\frac{96}{32}$ pt. = $3,000	1 pt. = $1,000
Treasury notes	CBOT	$100,000	$\frac{1}{32}$ pt. = $31.25	$\frac{64}{32}$ pt. = $2,000	1 pt. = $1,000
Treasury notes	IMM	$100,000	1 pt. = $15.625	48 pt. = $750	1 pt. = $15.625
Turkeys	CME	36,000 lbs.	2.5/100¢/lb = $9.00	1.5¢ = $540	1¢ = $360
Wheat	CBOT	5,000 bu.	$\frac{1}{4}$¢/bu. = $12.50	20¢ = $1,000	1¢ = $50
Wheat	KCBOT	5,000 bu.	$\frac{1}{4}$¢/bu. = $12.50	25¢ = $1,250	1¢ = $50
Wheat, durum	MGE	5,000 bu.	$\frac{1}{4}$¢c/bu. = $6.25	20¢ = $1,000	1¢ = $50
Wheat, spring	MGE	5,000 bu.	$\frac{1}{4}$¢/bu. = $6.25	20¢ = $1,000	1¢ = $50
Wheat	WCE	20 metric tons	10¢/ton = $2.00	$5 = $100	$1 = $20
Zinc	COMEX	60,000 lbs.	5/100¢/lb = $30.00	3¢ = $1,800	1¢ = $600

Commodity	Foreign Exchanges	Contract Size	Minimum Fluctuation
Aluminum	LME	25 metric tons	50 pence per metric ton
Barley	GAFTA	100 metric tons	0.05 pence per metric ton
Cocoa	LCT	10 metric tons	L 1.00 per metric ton
Coffee, Arabic	CTM	17,250 kg	5 cents per kilo
Coffee, robusta	CTM	5 metric tons	L 1.00 per metric ton
Copper cathodes	LME	25 metric tons	50 pence per metric ton
Copper wirebars	LME	25 metric tons	50 pence per metric ton
Gold	LBM	400 troy oz.	no minimum fluctuation
Lead	LME	25 metric tons	25 pence per metric ton

Commodity Contract Specifications—Foreign Exchanges

Commodity	Exchange	Contract Size	Minimum Fluctuation
Nickel	LME	6 metric tons	L 1.00
Palm oil	LVT	50 metric tons	25 pence per metric ton
Palladium		100 troy oz.	0.05 pence per troy oz.
Platinum		50 troy oz.	0.05 pence per troy oz.
Potatoes	GAFTA	40 metric tons	10 pence per metric ton
Rubber	LRT	15 metric tons	0.05 pence per kilogram
Silver	LME	10,000 troy oz.	0.01 pence per troy oz.
Silver bullion	LBM	5,000 troy oz.	0.01 pence per troy oz.
Soya bean meal	GAFTA	100 metric tons	10 pence per metric ton
Sugar no. 4	UTS	50 metric tons	0.05 pence per metric ton
Sugar, white	UTS	50 metric tons	0.05 pence per metric ton
Tin	LME	5 metric tons	L 1.00 per metric ton
Wheat	GAFTA	100 metric tons	0.05 pence per metric ton
Wool	LWT	2,500 kg.	0.1 pence per kilo
Zinc	LME	25 metric tons	25 pence per metric ton

Exchange Abbreviations:

CBT	Chicago Board of Trade
CME	Chicago Mercantile Exchange
CSCE	Coffee, Sugar, Cocoa Exchange
Comex	Commodity Exchange
IMM	International Monetary Market
KCBT	Kansas City Board of Trade
MGE	Minneapolis Grain Exchange
NYCE	New York Cotton Exchange
NYFE	New York Futures Exchange
NYME	New York Mercantile Exchange
WCE	Winnipeg Commodity Exchange
CTM	Coffee Terminal Market Assn. of London Ltd.
GAFTA	Grain & Feed Trade Assn.
LCT	London Cocoa Terminal Market Assn. Ltd.
LME	London Metal Exchange
LRT	London Rubber Terminal Market Assn. Ltd.
LWT	London Wool Terminal Market Assn. Ltd.
LVT	London Vegetable Oil Terminal Market Assn. Ltd.
UTS	United Terminal Sugar Market Assn. Ltd.

PART THREE

THE RULES AND REGULATIONS OF FUTURES TRADING

Introduction

Although it is a fast-paced market offering great rewards as well as risks, commodity futures trading is also a tightly structured and well-regulated industry. Part Three of the text reviews the internal and external controls that create a fair and efficient marketplace for today's commodity trader.

The first exchanges were chartered to provide efficient facilities where individuals interested in buying and selling futures contracts could offer, by open outcry, their price bids and offers. They were responsible for maintaining adequate communication devices to disseminate the buy and sell prices created in the trading pit. To fulfill this mandate, the exchanges established regulations and rules of conduct for their members. Violators faced suspension or revocation of their membership, fines and letters of warning, and, in some cases, disciplinary action under civil and federal law.

6

COMMODITY EXCHANGES: SELF-REGULATED INSTITUTIONS

Organizational Structure

The commodity exchanges specify the conditions of the futures contracts traded, enforce the integrity of the futures markets, and oversee the delivery function. The logistics for accomplishing these activities are developed by a board of directors served by several key committees.

Board of Directors

The board of directors is composed of exchange members. The membership body of the exchange elects the board and the board in turn selects an executive committee consisting of the president, vice-president, secretary, and chairman of the exchange. In addition to other activities, the executive committee hires exchange officials. These officials are paid staff people, usually nonmembers, who carry out the day-to-day operations at the exchange as directed by the board.

The board of directors and the executive committee also pass judgment on various regulations, hold hearings regarding violations, examine new contract markets, and plan for changes in the physical structure of the exchange. Much of the rudimentary work of the exchange's regulatory body is carried out by the committee structure.

Exchange Committees and Their Functions

Committees consisting of exchange members are primarily responsible for recommending rules and rule changes, hearing complaints, and anticipating problems.

Executive Committee	A liaison between staff management and board of directors to discuss policy decisions.
Arbitration Committee	Implements the exchange's arbitration rules and decides matters of controversy in accordance with those rules.
Business Conduct Committee	Supervises the business conduct of members, orders investigations, and holds hearing in connection with members' business conduct.
Clearinghouse Committee	Governs the operation of the clearinghouse.
Finance Committee	Reviews and directs the general administration of the exchange's financial affairs.
Membership Committee	Reviews applications for new members.
New Product/Business Development Committee	Oversees and establishes priorities with respect to the general development of the exchange's business, including new contracts, additional clearinghouse members, and marketing programs.
Orientation Committee	Conducts seminars to familiarize new members with federal requirements, exchange rules, and trading floor practices.
Pit Committee	Handles disputes occurring during the course of trading and deals with all matters which pertain to proper functioning of the pit. This committee also recommends the facilities needed in the pit area to accommodate members needs.
Rules Committee	Drafts new rules and suggests rule amendments.

Enforcement of Rules

One of the most active committees in the enforcement of rules is the Office for Investigations and Audits (OIA), responsible for auditing exchange members to ensure that they are maintaining their financial requirements and proper fiduciary qualifications. If OIA deems necessary, it can demand to review the books and bookkeeping systems of member futures commission merchants.

The OIA also investigates customer complaints, rule infractions, and improper conduct by exchange members. If a violation is uncovered by the OIA, the problem is referred to the appropriate committee or the board of directors for hearing. If judged guilty, the member is subject to one of several penalties, including a simple fine, a cease and desist order, liquidation of positions, or suspension or revocation of the membership seat. Members have the right to appeal to the board of directors, to the American Arbitration Association, or to government agencies, if applicable to the violation.

Membership on the Exchange

Becoming a member of an organized futures exchange involves more than simply paying a fee or purchasing a seat. To begin the membership application process, it is necessary to bid on a seat that is offered for sale; then the transfer of seats must be approved by the membership committee. After the buyer and seller have agreed to the sale price, the bid is formalized and the candidate must submit a written application for membership to the membership committee.

Membership application questions substantiate the identity, financial position, and moral character of the applicant. If approved, the applicant must attend an orientation program after which an examination may be given.

In many commodity exchanges, it is legal to lease a seat from an exchange member. The lessee and the lessor must gain approval of the membership committee, but the original seat owner is still responsible for the trades and any debits or misconduct of the lessee.

Exchange members have the right to vote in exchange elections, serve on committees, and hold official posts. These privileges, however, are ancillary to the financial advantages of owning an exchange seat.

Exchange members can conduct commodity futures contract transactions at the lowest possible commission rate. They have the privilege of trading for their own accounts on the exchange floor, so their only trading costs are the nominal clearing and exchange fees.

Another important reason to purchase an exchange seat is to speculate on the appreciation in its value. Seat values have escalated many times over the years, making exchange membership a solid financial investment; in fact, many members never trade on the exchange floor, preferring instead to hold the seat for its prestige and property value.

Registration of Commodity Representatives

Commodity exchanges require individuals involved in soliciting and handling customer accounts and funds to be registered as commodity representatives, also known as commodity brokers. The registration process involves filing an application with the exchanges and passing the National Commodity Futures Examination with a minimum score of 70. The test contains 125 questions on government and exchange regulations, mathematics of hedging, order writing, and other important areas.

Specific Exchange Regulations

Today there are 12 domestic commodity exchanges that are regulating more than 60 commodity futures contracts. Although there are slight variations in regulations among exchanges, they are generally uniform. The following rules and regulations are common to all the exchanges.

Discretionary Accounts

Discretionary accounts are opened by customers who wish to give a commodity representative responsibility for making trading decisions. Certain minimum standards must be met and maintained before a representative can take discretion in a customer's account. The minimum initial account size is currently $5,000 of beginning equity, but this is subject to change.

To handle discretionary accounts, the commodity representative must have power of attorney over the customer's trading account and the equity it represents. The representative must provide a special acknowledgment letter (rule 1990) to the commodity exchanges indicating that he or she has proper authority and limited power of attorney over the account. Upon approval, the customer is given a special account number for use by the commodity representative. Although customer authorization is not necessary to execute orders, confirmation of executed orders must be sent to the customer. If a customer wants to close a discretionary account, the power of attorney must be revoked, and revocation must be made in writing to the broker with confirmations to all participating parties. A commodity representative must have two years' experience before accepting a discretionary account, and proper supervision must be provided by the branch manager or an appropriate official of the brokerage office.

Investment companies can maintain customers for the purpose of conducting futures transactions through discretionary accounts such as managed accounts or limited partnership commodity funds, as long as proper reporting procedures are maintained. They must, however, file appropriate customer agreement forms and disclosure documents as prescribed by federal regulations. An investment company may also offer a circular or prospectus describing the nature of its business, the manner of trading, and a disclosure of risk to the customer.

In accordance with exchange regulations, the investment company must maintain 125 percent of the normal minimum margin requirement for customer protection purposes. Each participant in the investment company accounts must receive a monthly statement describing beginning and ending equity, trades, transactions, profits, losses, and commissions paid.

Approval of Advertising

All exchange members must have advertising relating to their commodity futures business approved by the commodity exchanges. Ordinarily, once one exchange grants approval, the others will waive their right to review the advertisement. The member can then publish the advertisement.

Commissions for Futures Transactions

On March 4, 1978, a federal law released controls on commission levels, allowing customers and their representatives to negotiate commissions for futures transactions at organized commodity exchanges. In many instances, this gave customers the right to negotiate lower commissions for reduced services. At certain commission levels, brokerage houses found that they did not need to provide market advice and specialized analysis to maintain satisfied customers. This ruling also gave brokerage houses the opportunity to increase commission levels for expanded services.

In contrast to securities transactions, commodity commissions are normally charged for the round turn and payable after a transaction is offset. Spread transactions usually require a lower commission than would be charged on each side of the transaction. Many brokerage offices offer lower commissions to trade (hedge) customers than to their speculative customers because hedgers are thought to have greater financial stability and are more likely to trade in large orders.

When changing brokerage offices, the customer may choose to have market positions transferred rather than offset. In this case, the original brokerage would charge commissions on the positions and the new office would accept them without commission charges as a courtesy to the customer. Decisions regarding commissions on the transfer of positions from one office to another are left to the discretion of the brokerage houses. Like commission fees, these transactions are open to negotiation.

Exchange Employee Accounts

Many commodity exchanges do not allow their employees to trade or hold positions in the futures market. Special approval must be granted, and employee accounts are subject to the same scrutiny as exchange member accounts under the auspices of the OIA.

Punishable Exchange Rule Violations

Punishment for exchange rule violations depends on the severity of the offense. Activities that interfere with the function and economic purpose of the commodity futures market or that detract from its integrity are considered major offenses. These include fictitious trading, circulation of false rumors, default on a futures contract, and failure to maintain minimum financial net worth.

Fictitious Trading

Fictitious trading includes the fraudulent activity called *bucketing of orders*. The term refers to the practice of accepting client orders that are not placed with the commodity exchange but are simply held by the representative. The representative may be tempted to accept equal but opposite orders from two customers, knowing that if one loses money the other will make money. He can simply transfer capital from one customer to the other, thereby avoiding the cost of executing the futures position.

Another example of fictitious trading would involve telling a customer that orders have been made, executed, and offset on his or her behalf, and that the customer has supposedly lost money or broken even on market price change. The representative charges a commission fee even though no futures trade has actually been made. Since this could be a post-market activity, it would be very difficult for the customer to know whether or not the orders were actually placed without examining computer trade confirmations. The representative profits from the customer's "losing trade" while securing a round turn commission.

Generally, fictitious trading involves transactions that are purported to have been executed in the futures market but in fact were not. Punishments for fictitious trading range from monetary fines to suspension of membership privileges. Some offenses fall under the jurisdiction of the Commodity Futures Trading Commission as federal rule violations.

Circulation of False Rumors

Although this rule involves the somewhat grey area of truth and fact, blatantly false rumors are readily detectible. An exchange member or investor could benefit financially from the short-term disruption caused by such rumors as the death of a national leader, a military attack, or a major shift in supply or demand for a vital commodity. The punishment for circulating false rumors is commensurate with the severity of its effect on the market, but it usually entails returning the financial gain to the injured parties.

Default on a Futures Contract

All customers trading commodity futures must sign an agreement stating that they accept the conditions of the commodity contracts within which they have placed orders and accepted positions. Default on a futures contract—by refusing to accept or make delivery, by delivering unsuitable quality, or by failing to observe contract specifications—is a serious violation of both exchange and federal regulations.

Failure to Maintain Minimum Financial Net Worth

Minimum financial net worth regulations apply to certain members and activities in the futures markets, such as the minimum financial net worth required for member and nonmember futures commission merchants. FCMs are required to maintain a minimum financial net worth because they must guarantee payments to the clearinghouse for customer market losses through the payment of variable margins as described later in this chapter. Failure to maintain the proper financial net worth is likely to result in suspension of trading privileges until minimums are met. These net worth requirements are separate from the customer's segregated funds and act as guarantee that if insufficient customer funds are available, the FCM's financial net worth would protect from default. Net worth requirements are higher for exchange members than for nonmember FCMs.

Minor Offenses

Minor violations are those that do not jeopardize customer funds or the general integrity of the futures markets. They usually involve unbusinesslike conduct or errors in judgment.

Errors and Adjustments

Once a trade is made, the price is binding. In the fast-paced activity of order delivery, acceptance, and pit trading, orders are sometimes misinterpreted. In the urgency to satisfy a customer's request, a commodity representative may misunderstand the specifications: A customer may have given an order to buy 5,000 March corn, but the commodity representative may have understood buy 5,000 May corn. For this reason, the customer's order is repeated to the customer before it is entered in the market.

In the event that an erroneous order is placed in the commodity futures markets and executed in the pits, the trade cannot be changed in any fashion but must stand as a legitimate transaction until offset. If a loss is incurred in the process of offsetting an erroneous order and initiating a corrected one, the violating party is responsible for that loss. If the order was improperly filled by the pit broker, the pit broker must compensate the customer for financial damages. If the commodity representative misinterpreted the order, then the representative is responsible for reparations. The brokerage office often accepts responsibility for representatives' errors while seeking to avoid future errors.

Margins

Earlier in this book, margins were described as a security or performance bond designed to ensure the integrity and performance of a commodity futures contract. Margins should never be considered a down payment or a partial payment on the contract. A down payment implies ownership with a liability to pay full value, whereas margin guarantees the performance of the person assuming a contractual position.

If conditions relating to the volatility or value of the futures contract change, the exchange may raise or lower the margin. If a commodity's price levels become more volatile, the exchange may feel justified in increasing the margin or performance bond. If prices for a particular commodity rise over a period of time, thus increasing its overall value, larger performance bonds may be required to secure a market position. Conversely, lower prices and a more stable market may induce the exchange to reduce margins on a commodity.

In establishing margin levels, the exchange's regulating body takes into account:

- the total value of the commodity represented by the futures contract
- the amount of price movement allowed in a single trading day
- the price volatility, in a single day and over a period of time
- the closeness to the delivery period

It is important to remember that the margins are set by the commodity exchanges and not by an outside regulatory body such as the Commodity Futures Trading Commission.

When the exchange establishes margins, it sets initial as well as maintenance levels. Maintenance margin is the amount of performance bond required to maintain a futures position after it is initiated (usually 80 percent of initial margin). In signing the agreement form, the customer promises to maintain minimum margin levels. Failure to do so gives the futures commission merchant's brokerage office the right to liquidate his or her positions. If the margin account is in deficit, the office may ask the customer to provide funds beyond the amount that was originally established as margin.

To initiate a futures position, initial margin must be available at the time of market entry. As long as price activity does not cause the equity balance in the customer's account to fall below the minimum maintenance margin level, the account needs no additional capital. Once trade equity declines below that level, the customer must bring the account back to initial margin by depositing more capital.

Property Instead of Cash for Margins

In a very limited way, property other than cash can be used for margins. This includes government securities (Treasury bills) or, in some instances, exchange stock for the exchange within which the market position is held. If allowed, these properties can be used only for maintenance margins; initial margin must be in cash.

Spread and Hedge Margins

Margins on lower risk positions are generally lower. A position in the futures market that involves a long position and a short position in the same commodity but two different delivery months is called a *spread* and generally requires a lower margin than a net position or a single long or a single short position in the same commodity. Prices of delivery months tend to move in a parallel fashion, thereby reducing risk. In cases where wide aberrations are likely to occur between delivery months, as with months in different crop years, the exchange will usually set a higher spread margin level.

Margins for bona fide hedge customers (also called *trade* customers) are typically lower for the same reason that spread margins are less than margins on open positions. The bona fide hedger has a cash position that balances the futures position. In trying to hedge the value of an inventory of commodity, the hedger can assume a short position in the futures market; loss in the futures position due to price increases will generally be compensated by a gain in the inventory value.

A hedge is a spread between cash and futures rather than within futures options or markets. In both hedge and spread transactions, equal and opposite positions tend to offset one another. A hedge is considered secured by the customer's cash inventory and, therefore, requires less margin. For example, a long hedger may protect against a price increase of a commodity that will be purchased in the future. Should the price fall, the cheaper cash purchase price offsets losses in the long futures position.

Variation Margin and Clearinghouse Members

When a clearinghouse member takes on the responsibility of clearing trades for customers, he has an obligation to maintain margin levels that are appropriate for each customer's positions. If market action produces losses in any positions, the clearinghouse member must restore them to a full margined level. The settlement price on the day in question determines the amount necessary to bring a position back to margin. The clearinghouse member must then deposit the necessary capital prior to the opening of trading the following day.

If market activity during the trading day demands deposit of capital to satisfy a deficit prior to market closing, the exchange will require the clearinghouse to deposit variation margin within one hour. A one-hour demand is unusual, but it can occur. Generally, short notice demands for capital are easily met by clearinghouse members through wire transfer of funds. Through the same mechanism of wire transfer, a clearinghouse member can request, on a daily basis, that surpluses in margin accounts be wired to an interest-bearing account at a bank, enabling the FCM to earn overnight interest on unused capital.

Segregated Funds

Futures clearing merchants must keep their operating capital separate from customer funds. The segregated funds rule maintains the integrity of the market by protecting the customer's funds from mismanagement and by guaranteeing the availability of those funds if losses occur in the account or the FCM experiences financial difficulty.

Delivery Procedures

Once a market has moved into a delivery period, the seller has the right to execute delivery of the commodity. The definition of a deliverable position varies according to individual contract specifications. Generally, it means that a commodity is in an appropriate place for delivery at a bonded warehouse or vault and has been graded or inspected to meet the specifications of the contract. Once these criteria are met, the seller can execute a notice of intent to deliver through the clearinghouse member representing the customer's account.

The seller provides notice of intent to deliver to the bookkeeping division of the clearinghouse. The clearinghouse then has to find the oldest net long. The oldest net long receives the notice of intent to deliver accompanied by a warehouse receipt or other negotiated instrument. Upon notification, the customer holding the long position can either liquidate the position, thereby avoiding delivery, or retender delivery by taking a short position in the futures market and executing his or her own intention to deliver. If the buyer accepts delivery, he or she pays the clearinghouse member, who in turn pays the clearinghouse; the clearinghouse then pays the seller.

If an inspection certificate is used in delivery, the exchange will appoint an inspector or a qualified agency to grade the commodity. The buyer has the option of accepting the inspection certificate or requesting a new one. In some instances, the buyer may request a sample of the commodity before accepting delivery.

It is the delivery process that separates gambling from speculating in futures contracts. Without the assurance that the delivery of an actual commodity can result from assuming a contractual position in the futures markets, these markets would have no relation to the real world. As mentioned earlier, default on delivery is a serious offense that carries a severe penalty.

Daily Price Fluctuations Limits

It is a major responsibility of the commodity exchanges to maintain an orderly market. Orderly markets foster participation and ensure that customers with profitable positions will receive the profits provided by the losses of customers with losing positions.

Daily price limits are imposed to ensure that the clearinghouse member, the VCV, or the FCM has time to seek out additional capital from customers during times of violent price activity. A daily price limit is the maximum price change that can occur in a single trading day. This change is calculated from the previous day's settlement price and dictates the maximum price movement, both up and down. Once a limit is met, either on the high side or the low side, trading can continue at that limit, but no prices can be made beyond it.

Price limits vary by commodity and are set by the exchanges. If a market moves to the limit for a given number of days, some exchanges increase the limit value; others permit the limit to be lifted altogether. Nearby or spot delivery months in commodity futures contracts usually have no limits because they are closest to the cash market activity and may fluctuate freely with the cash price.

Orders—The Communication to the Trading Pits

Exchanges provide an auction market where bid and ask prices are established by open outcry. This auction determines commodity prices and ensures that bids and asks reach the widest possible audience. The urgency and aggressiveness of the buyers and sellers move prices up or down within the market system. Orders must be placed by open outcry to prevent special arrangements between brokers and traders without the detection of exchange authorities.

Floor brokers must keep customer orders confidential until they are filled by open outcry. They may not fill orders away from the trading pit or outside of specific trading hours. Once an order is filled, the customer must receive confirmation of its execution.

When floor brokers are trading for their own accounts, the clearinghouse computers receive their daily order cards so that they can be matched with opposite orders.

Commodity Order Writing

Orders are communications to the floor broker. The action in the trading pit is fast and furious, leaving no time to second guess what is meant by an improperly written order. If the floor broker does not understand an order, he may fill it improperly or return it unfilled. Whether you are a commodity trader or a representative, it is important to you and your profits that your order give accurate and complete information to the floor broker.

Following are various types of orders and guidelines for using them effectively.

Market Order

The most common order in the commodities arena is the market order. As the name implies, the market order is to be filled at the market price at the time it reaches the pit.

Suppose a speculator feels that the December corn price will decline and decides to go short 5,000 bushels. This individual is anxious to enter the market and would be satisfied at the present price of $2.60. An order to "sell 5 Dec. corn at the market" would be filled at the prevailing market price when it reached the pit. Even though the speculator would be satisfied with $2.60, the market may fluctuate before the order reaches the pit. In these cases, the order will be filled at the price that prevails when it arrives (Figure 6.1).

Limit Order

A limit order, sometimes called a price order, states a specific price such as "sell 5 Dec. corn at $2.70." This tells the floor broker to sell 5,000 bushels of December corn at $2.70 or better. It would not be properly filled at $2.69 but could be filled at $2.71, since that is a better price for a short position than $2.70 (Figure 6.2).

Because a trader normally places limit orders to obtain a better

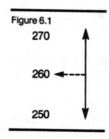

Figure 6.1

270

260

250

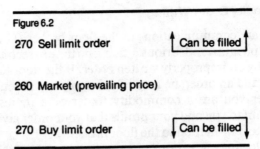

Figure 6.2

270 Sell limit order   Can be filled

260 Market (prevailing price)

270 Buy limit order   Can be filled

than prevailing market price, a limit order to sell is always placed above the prevailing market price and a limit order to buy is always placed below the prevailing market price (Figure 6.3).

The expression "or better" is understood in a limit order. Do not place OB after the price of a limit order unless you want to place a sell limit order below the prevailing market. OB tells a floor broker that you know the present market price is better than the price you designate but that you are willing to give the broker a little latitude in executing the order.

Assume that the present market price of $2.60 is a good place to buy corn futures but that the market is also volatile in this price area. Fearing that a market order would result in a "bad fill," a speculator might enter the market with an order to "buy Dec. corn at $2.65 OB."

This tells the floor broker that the speculator is willing to give the market a little latitude but wants to limit exposure to its volatility. There is no question that this is a legitimate order, even though it

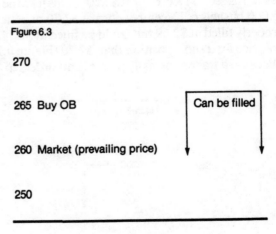

Figure 6.3

270

265 Buy OB   Can be filled

260 Market (prevailing price)

250

is above the market. The broker will not think that a sell order has been mislabeled or that a different price or option month was intended.

Stop Order

Stop orders tell the floor broker to stop what he or she is doing and fill the order if the price is hit. Buy stop orders are always placed above the prevailing market price; sell stop orders are always placed below market price. Once the stop price is hit, the order is filled as a market order.

Take the example of an order to "sell 5 Dec. corn $2.50 stop." The market price is at $2.60. If the price declines to $2.50 and hits the stop price, then this should be filled as a market order. A sell stop at $2.50 could be filled at $2.65 or $2.45 since it is a market order once the stop price is hit (Figure 6.4).

Market if Touched Order

Market if touched orders (MITS) are like stop orders. They demand immediate action from the floor broker when the designated price is hit; the order is then filled as a market order. A fundamental difference between a stop order and an MIT is that a sell MIT is placed above rather than below the prevailing market price. Once the price is hit, the MIT is filled as a market order (Figure 6.5).

Stop Limit Order

Stop limit orders combine the characteristics of a stop order and a limit order. The stop price of a stop limit order is the first consideration of the floor broker. A stop limit order to buy is placed above the prevailing market price and a stop limit order to sell is placed below that price. If this price is hit, then the order is to be filled as a limit order (Figure 6.6).

Suppose a speculator is interested in being short 5 December corn at $2.50 but is afraid that once the price reaches that level it will

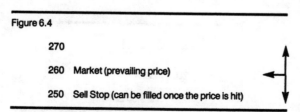

Figure 6.4

270

260   Market (prevailing price)

250   Sell Stop (can be filled once the price is hit)

Figure 6.5

270 Sell MIT

260 Market (prevailing price)

250 Buy MIT

---

rapidly decline. To take a short position at $2.50 or better, the speculator would place an order to "sell 5 Dec. corn at $2.50 stop limit." If the prevailing market is $2.60 and declines to $2.50, the stop is activated, which means that the order can be filled at $2.50 or better but cannot be filled at $2.49 or lower (Figure 6.7).

In a stop limit order, the stop price can differ. If an order directs a broker to "sell 5 Dec. corn at $2.50 stop $2.48 limit," the market would activate the order at $2.50 stop and then would have a two-cent latitude on the down side of the fill. (See Figure 6.8.)

Fill or Kill

Sometimes called a quick order, the fill or kill is offered to the floor once, twice, or maybe three times. If it is not filled, it is canceled.

One Cancels the Other (OCO)

This may be a buy order and a sell order placed in the market at the same time; when one is filled, the other is canceled. This order can bracket a trading range and will automatically put the trader into the market on the side of the breakout.

The Cancel Order

An order can be sent into the pit to cancel one that has already been placed. Obviously, an order cannot be canceled once it has been filled.

Figure 6.6

270 Buy Stop Limit

260 Market

250 Sell Stop Limit

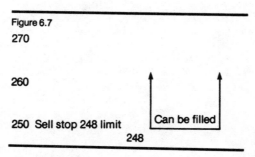

Figure 6.7

Open Order or Good till Canceled (GTC)

Open orders remain in effect until they are canceled or the contract expires. Orders that are not designated as good till canceled are treated as day orders.

Stop Spread

A stop spread is a variation on the spread order. A spread order calls for the broker to buy one contract and to sell another in the futures market. A spread stop indicates the buy-sell price differential desired by the customer. It also stipulates that when the differential is hit, the order is to be filled as a market spread.

If a broker receives an order to liquidate a position, the position being offset is always the oldest one unless otherwise indicated. For example, a customer is long two gold contracts on July 1 and long two gold contracts on July 2. If on July 3 he executes an order to buy two gold contracts to offset an existing position, that will automatically be the July 1 position.

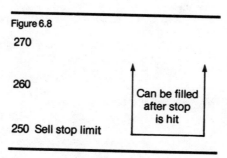

Figure 6.8

7

GOVERNMENT REGULATIONS AS PRESCRIBED BY THE COMMODITY FUTURES TRADING COMMISSION

The Evolution of the Commodity Futures Trading Commission

From the beginning of commodity futures trading in the United States in the mid-1800s, the industry has been largely self-regulated. Commodity exchanges developed their own set of rules to keep their markets free from undue outside regulation. Exchange rules protect against market manipulation, default on contracts, and other fraudulent or destructive activities.

Even the earliest involvement of the federal government in regulating the futures industry, the Grain Futures Act of 1922, was for the most part in harmony with exchange regulations. Renamed the Commodity Exchange Act in 1936, it placed the burden of regulation in the futures industry on the exchanges. The Commodity Exchange Authority (CEA) authorized under this act was primarily a supervisory governmental body. It worked in cooperation with the exchanges to keep the industry free of manipulation.

The CEA was placed within the Department of Agriculture, where it was somewhat dwarfed. With a small staff and limited funds, the CEA often relied on other government agencies to perform its tasks. For example, the CEA could not take a violator to court. If it suspected a rule violation, it would pass the information on to the Justice Department, which would injuncture, indict, or file suit. Overall, the major shortcoming of the CEA was that its rules lacked teeth.

Commodity Futures Trading Act

Even with its limited staff, the CEA managed to enforce major trading regulations. Prior to 1972, it kept criminal acts under control and followed up on occasional complaints from individuals injured by violators of exchange regulations.

A chain of weather-related events in the early 1970s had a major impact on world grain markets. Early frost in some parts of the Midwest in the fall of 1972 damaged corn crops, and snows buried enough of the soybean crop to launch a bull market. Meanwhile, halfway around the world, Russia experienced a major wheat crop failure. While a wet spring and flooding in the Delta region of the United States delayed plantings, Russia purchased large quantities of wheat, corn, and soybeans from American grain companies to secure its supplies against another crop failure. At the same time, off the coast of Peru, the Humboldt Current shifted, changing the water temperatures, reducing the fish population and curtailing Peru's major export, fishmeal, a protein supplement used for cattle feed in countries around the world. Without fishmeal, the world's cattle feeders quickly turned to soybeans as an alternate source of protein.

These natural events converged to cause unexpected shortages and an unprecedented rally in world grain prices. This dramatic rise in food prices disrupted futures. As prices climb, so do the profits of those who own and produce the commodity. In the futures industry, however, rising prices bring profits to the buyers or long positions in the market and losses to the sellers or short positions. The skyrocketing prices of 1972-1973 brought a cry of agony from those who held short positions, mainly producers and farmers, who felt that someone had taken unfair advantage of them.

Congressional hearings were convened to review complaints from injured parties and to scrutinize the ruling bodies of the futures industry, in particular the CEA and the commodity exchanges. Legislators questioned the adequacy of self-regulation and many thought that the federal government should exert greater control over the industry. Meanwhile, the CEA had its hands full filing memoranda to the Justice Department to pursue legal action against serious violators. Unfortunately, the Justice Department was also busy—dealing with the Watergate hearings.

The unusual chain of events—high grain prices, increased commodity market activity, and public demand for reform and regulation—led to passage of the Commodity Futures Trading Act of 1974.

The Role of the Commodity Futures Trading Commission

The Commodity Futures Trading Act of 1974 was a dramatic revision of the Commodity Exchange Act of 1936. A major part of that revision replaced the Commodity Exchange Authority with the Commodity Futures Trading Commission (CFTC). The commission gained exclusive jurisdiction aver all activities taking place in organized commodity futures exchanges. It also received the legal muscle to indict, injunction, and hold criminal proceedings. With the creation of the CFTC, the U.S. government took a major step toward imposing federal regulation on commodity futures trading activity.

The Commodity Futures Trading Act of 1974 gave the CFTC two main functions:

- to protect and improve the price and hedging function of the futures market
- to protect investors in the futures market

CFTC regulation came in two forms: oversight regulation for exchange activities, and direct regulation through registration of individuals with fiduciary responsibility to futures customers.

Oversight Regulation

The authors of the 1974 act felt that the CEA was ineffective in its attempts to enforce the rules established by the commodities exchanges, so they empowered the CFTC to monitor exchange activities and regulations. Oversight responsibilities of the CFTC include: contract market designation, approval of exchange rules, and examination of accounting records.

Contract Market Designation

Under the new legislation, commodity exchanges must gain CFTC approval before developing and implementing new contract markets. The exchanges must give sufficient economic justification for the new contracts and must show that they will serve the industries that produce and use the commodity. The CFTC can control the growth of futures markets by simply delaying or expediting the approval of new contract markets.

Approval of Exchange Rules

The previous chapter pointed out that commodity exchanges differ from one another in the specifics of their regulations. The

CFTC has responsibility for examining the regulations of each exchange. It does not dictate what their rules should be but will often specify minimum standards, such as a financial requirement for futures commission merchants. This supervisory function allows the exchanges some flexibility while enabling the CFTC to have input without intervention.

Examination of Accounting Records

Accounting records of fiduciary participants in the commodity futures industry fall under the jurisdiction of the CFTC. The commission can and will audit the books and accounting procedures of commodities exchanges and their member and nonmember FCMs. The Office of Investigation and Audits within the exchanges performs a similar task.

Direct Regulation

One very specific way the CFTC provides direct regulation to the commodity futures industry is through the registration of fiduciaries and other participants who handle customer money. This includes five groups of individuals and organizations.

Futures Commission Merchants (FCM)

Both member and nonmember futures commission merchants must register with the CFTC every two years. To be approved ,futures commission merchants must be able to show a financial net worth of at least $50,000. Actually, most commodity exchanges require a larger net worth minimum than the CFTC. This is permissible, but they must not allow FCMs to be below the minimums.

As an added protection for the customer, the FCM must also segregate customer funds from operating capital. If the FCM encountered financial difficulty, customer funds would remain intact and available. The FCM must make financial reports both to its customers and to the CFTC. Reports to customers include: confirmation of trades, profit and loss statements, and monthly trading activity summaries.

The CFTC also requires that the FCM maintain accurate records of customer account activities, a proper accounting of the customer segregated funds, and records of trade confirmations, including copies of time-stamped orders and individual customer statements. The FCM's books must be ready for a CFTC audit at all times.

Associated Persons

The associated persons category is made up primarily of registered commodity representatives, but it also includes sales assistants and branch office managers. Associated persons must file an 8R form every two years and must be registered under the auspices of a registered FCM.

Floor Brokers

To trade on a commodity exchange floor, an individual must represent a member of the exchange. A membership may be purchased or leased, but the individual must file an 8R application with the CFTC before trading on the exchange. A floor trader must also register every two years as an associated person.

Commodity Trading Advisors

Before managing a futures trading account for a customer, an individual or company must register as a commodity trading advisor. This involves filing an 8R form every year with the appropriate amendment.

Commodity Pool Operators

Commodity pool operators draw together the trading equity of several customers, combine those equities into a single account, and then trade that account as one. They might also combine funds to form a commodity limited partnership fund. These individuals must register with the CFTC every year.

Customer Protection Rules

The 1974 commodity act incorporated important customer protection rules. It requires that all customers establishing accounts to trade commodity futures know the risks involved and have their best interests protected. Customers must read and sign a risk disclosure statement when establishing a trading account.

The act also prohibits unauthorized trading. Unauthorized trading would occur if a broker, without the knowledge and written permission of a customer, were to establish positions in the futures market on that person's behalf. To prevent this, the CFTC requires appropriate reports for each commodity futures customer. As an added protection, the branch manager or someone in a similar position must supervise all associated persons' activities.

The FCM must also file large trader reports providing information on the size of positions held by large speculators and hedgers. When they exceed designated limits, speculators and hedgers must file a report—a separate one for every commodity on which they exceed the limit. Reportable limits may be adjusted by the CFTC if the size of the contract market increases or decreases markedly.

Many futures markets have speculative limits set by the CFTC and, in some cases, the commodity exchanges. These limits specify the maximum number of contracts that speculators may control. Calculation of maximum position size varies slightly among commodities. In some instances, a net position is indicated as having a limit; in others, limits refer to a maximum number of contracts for each delivery month. In any case, speculators must fall within the limit at the close of each trading session. They might trade and hold a position greater than a speculative limit during market hours but must reduce their position to the limit before closing if they wish to retain it overnight.

Only bona fide hedgers may disregard speculative limits as long as their futures position is less than or equal to their cash market. Hedgers who hold positions larger than their cash market needs fall under the jurisdiction of the speculative limit rule.

Speculative limits and reportable levels are as follows:

Commodity	CFTC Reporting Levels	Speculative Position Limits
Wheat		
Winter	500,000 bushels	3,000,000 bu. net, no more than 3,000,000 bu. any month
Spring	500,000 bushels	3,000,000 bu. net, no more than 3,000,000 bu. any month
Durum	500,000 bushels	3,000,000 net combined
Corn	500,000 bushels	3,000,000 bu. any or all months
Oats	200,000 bushels	2,000,000 bu. for spec. 3,000,000 bu. if 1,000,000 bu. is a spread
Soybeans	500,000 bushels	3,000,000 bu. any or all months
Soybean oil	100 contracts	540 contracts combined
Soybean meal	100 contracts	720 contracts combined
Cotton	5,000 bales	30,000 bales
Cattle		
Live	100 contracts	300 contracts long or short in any delivery month

Feeder	25 contracts	300 contracts long or short in any delivery month
Hogs	50 contracts	750 contracts total long or short with no more than 300 in a single month
Pork bellies	25 contracts	250 contracts net total Maximum of 150 Feb., 150 Mar., 200 May, 150 July, 150 Aug.
Potatoes	25 contracts	300 carlots any month, 350 all months
Sugar	50 contracts	*
Silver bullion	250 contracts	*
Copper	100 contracts	*
Gold	100 contracts	*
Platinum	25 contracts	*
Foreign currencies	25 contracts	*
U.S. bonds	100 contracts	*
U.S. T-bills	25 contracts	*
GNMAs	100 contracts	*
All other commodities	25 contracts	*

*Regulated by exchanges.

CFTC Investigations and Enforcement Activities

As mentioned earlier, the CFTC can audit futures market participants and investigate their activities if there is reasonable suspicion of wrongdoing. If it finds evidence that an individual or company is in violation of a rule, it may require a formal hearing or even bring criminal proceedings. Although it handles most minor violations with letters of warning, CFTC penalties can include large fines or suspension from trading activity.

National Futures Association

The Commodity Futures Trading Act mandated the CFTC to spearhead the establishment of a National Futures Association (NFA) that would perform a function similar to that of the National Association of Security Dealers (NASD) in the securities industry. The NFA would construct certification tests and create a self-regulated membership body of individuals involved in the futures industry. The organization would foster unity in the industry by standardizing regulations and testing procedures.

8

FUTURES COMMISSION MERCHANT PROCEDURAL HANDBOOK

FCM Guidelines—An Approach to Self-Regulation

Exchange and government rules form the core of futures regulation, but they are not the only controls. Each FCM picks up where the formal regulations leave off by prescribing unique rules and operational procedures for itself and its clients.

Some FCMs formalize their regulations in a handbook; others pass them along in training sessions and memoranda. In either case, nearly all have regulations that meet or exceed the standards set out by the exchanges and the federal government. The following is a sample procedural handbook consolidated from the handbooks of many different FCMs.

Handling Accounts

New Accounts

In order to confine speculative commodity business to those who can afford the risks, branch managers are required to review the customer's financial position before opening an account. They should be satisfied that the customer is ready, willing, and able to undertake the risks involved in the commodity markets. Customers with a small equity base to trade (i.e., those who meet only minimum account requirements) have less chance of success and thus should be discouraged from the start.

Before approving new accounts, the branch manager must confirm that a customer can afford to risk at least three times the maximum amount of margin that he or she commits to the markets. Even the smallest accounts should be able to risk at least $15,000. A new account must have $5,000 deposited before trading can begin. If deposit is made by check, the check must clear prior to trading. Further, the loss of this risk capital should not seriously affect a customer's financial position, standard of living, or ability to support dependents. Branch managers should also review the more general suitability of the customer in terms of income, sophistication, and general knowledge of commodities.

Ineligible Accounts

Accounts for minors, directly or through custodians or guardians, are normally not accepted. Exceptions are trusts, estates, ERISA accounts, and third-party accounts which the branch manager must approve in advance, in writing. The branch manager will review all accompanying documents—such as trust indenture agreements—to make sure that speculation in a commodity account falls within the powers given to trustees or executors.

Discretionary Accounts

The branch manager will approve discretionary accounts after answering the following questions:

- Why is the customer giving discretion?
- Who is receiving discretion—a third party or a commodity representative?
- If a third party, what is the relation to the customer?
- If a commodity representative, has he or she been registered for at least two years in accordance with exchange rules?
- Is the customer financially able and willing to maintain at least $5,000 in the account at all times in accordance with exchange rules?
- Does the branch manager understand that all orders must be reviewed and initialed each day in accordance with exchange rules?
- Does the branch manager understand that the account must be reviewed frequently for signs of overtrading?
- Have arrangements been made to provide each member of a discretionary account with a monthly statement?

- Are all account papers signed and in hand, including the risk disclosure statement?
- Has the customer received an oral explanation of risks such as limit moves, as prescribed by the CFTC?
- If the third party is a commodity pool operator or commodity trading advisor, does the branch manager have a copy of the CFTC registration on file?
- Does the customer understand that a new power of attorney must be obtained each year?

No trades should be made until written approval of the account is received from the branch manager.

Employee Accounts

Employees are not encouraged to have commodity accounts, but those who do should follow these guidelines:

- Employees may not trade for their own accounts if they owe the firm money due to errors or deficits. They must meet minimum net worth and income requirements in order to open an account.
- Employees must avoid excessive trading activity. The management team will review their accounts periodically.
- Personal trading must not interfere with performance of normal duties. If it consumes too much time, trading privileges will be revoked. The right is reserved to close out any employee position which the branch manager deems detrimental to the firm.
- Margin calls must be met within 24 hours, regardless of commissions due the employee. Commissions due will not be applied to offset margin calls.
- The customer always comes first. Customer orders must be time-stamped, entered, and executed before employee orders.

Segregated and Nonsegregated Accounts

CFTC regulations require that all customer commodity funds be segregated from firm funds. These regulations apply only to commodities traded on domestic markets and require that the margin funds received for such trades be placed in the customer's segregated account.

If a customer begins trading in foreign commodities (e.g., Winnipeg gold, London cocoa), a nonsegregated account will be opened using the same account number as the segregated one. All such trades will be shown in this nonsegregated account, and all statements will clearly designate the type of account.

The nonsegregated account is also for delivery of a commodity. When the futures contract is converted into receipt or delivery of a cash commodity, funds are placed in the nonsegregated account. Thereupon, transactions involving the cash commodity are recorded in this account.

Each branch office must have two bank accounts for commodities. One should be designated "Customers' Segregated Funds" and the other "Nonsegregated Funds." Each branch office must retain in its files an acknowledgment from its bank stating that the bank has been informed that the deposits are from a commodity customer and are being segregated in compliance with the Commodity Futures Trading Act.

Commodity Account Forms

The following indicates what forms are required to open each type of account. The broker and branch manager should ensure that forms are properly completed. Copies of many of these forms can be found in Appendix D.

Individual Account

Customer agreement
Supplemental customer agreement
Risk disclosure statement

Joint Account or Partnership Account

Customer agreement
Supplemental customer agreement
Risk disclosure statement
Joint account agreement

Limited Partnership Account

Customer agreement
Supplemental customer agreement
Risk disclosure statement
Limited partnership agreement

Corporate Account

Customer agreement
Risk disclosure statement
Corporate account agreement and resolution form
Supplemental customer agreement

Pension Plans

Customer agreement
Supplemental customer agreement
Risk disclosure agreement
Copy of the plan indicating trustee(s) authority to trade commodities

Trust Plans

Customer agreement
Supplemental customer agreement
Risk disclosure statement
Copy of the plan indicating trustee(s) authority to trade commodities

Managed Commodity Accounts

Customer agreement
Supplemental customer agreement
Risk disclosure statement
Trading authorization limited to purchase and sale of commodities
Supplement to manage account trading authorization
Advisors agreement

Hedge Account

Because any of the four general types of accounts could be hedge accounts, the hedge form should be included with the other required forms. Customers who have been approved for hedge accounts should use them to trade only those commodities which relate to their hedge approval. Other commodities should be traded in a separate speculative account.

Broker and Third-Party Discretionary Accounts

Because any of the four general types of accounts could be broker or third-party discretionary accounts, the third-party power of attorney form should be included with the other required forms, if appropriate. No account can be opened with a person affiliated with another futures commission merchant unless written authorization is received from a person designated by the FCM to oversee the employee's account. Also, copies of all confirmations originating in the account must be sent to the FCM as the transactions occur. No account can be opened with a person affiliated with a bank, financial institution, or any broker/dealer registered under the SEC acts of 1933, 1934, 1940, or subsequent revisions thereof unless written approval is received from an officer of said company.

All commodities records must be retained for five years and be readily accessible for at least the first two of these years.

Investment Club Accounts

It is the responsibility of each commodity representative who handles a club or other combination account to see that each member of the group receives a monthly statement.

Margins

Before initiating a position in the commodity futures markets, a customer is required to deposit initial margin against the contract value. Since futures contracts contemplate physical delivery at some future date, the full value of a contract is not due or required until delivery time. Initial margin requirements are usually 5 to 15 percent of the full value of the contract.

If market action impairs about 20 percent of the initial margin, the customer must immediately deposit an amount equal to the loss. In other words, if account equity falls below the maintenance margin level (generally about 80 percent of initial margin), the customer must promptly deposit sufficient funds to bring the equity back up to the initial margin level.

The FCM must deposit initial margins with the clearinghouse of each exchange. Every day, the clearinghouses mark to the market all positions and deposit the full amount of any losses due to that day's price fluctuations in customers' accounts. The FCM will place a margin call only when equity in any account falls below the maintenance margin level rather than calling a customer on a same-day basis like the clearinghouses. Customers are expected to make prompt deposits when given a margin call because funds have already been advanced to the clearinghouse. Failure to collect margins promptly can be a serious problem for FCMs and can increase the possibility of deficits or unsecured debits in customers' accounts.

A commodity representative who adheres to the requirements

for opening new accounts and follows businesslike procedures in the handling of margins can avoid problems in conducting commodity business. Margins are the primary protection against losses due to bad debts. Remember, margin calls always precede deficits.

Margin Schedules

The FCM can revise and republish margin schedules, but margin rates may change without notice. Moreover, these changes may be made retroactively. The FCM reserves the right to ask customers for additional margins at any time it deems appropriate.

The margin schedule reflects two different rates. As a matter of policy, all speculative accounts are charged the regular margin rate. Hedge margins are reserved for customers who have submitted hedge letters and for trades that are bona fide hedge transactions.

A margin call is issued when margin requirements are greater than the customer's equity. Initial margin requirements for all new positions may be satisfied by:

- prompt deposit of cash
- liquidation of previously held, fully margined positions within 24 hours of the issuance of the call (This will be considered as satisfaction of an initial margin call to the extent that such liquidation reduces the initial margin requirements in the account so that the equity is at least equal to the new margin requirements.)

Maintenance Margin

A maintenance call results when the equity in the account falls approximately 20 percent below the initial margin requirement. The customer may meet this call by depositing cash, spreading the position, or by liquidating positions.

Cash Commodity

If an account has taken delivery of a cash commodity and paid for the contract, and if the FCM is holding a warehouse receipt for that commodity, then the value of the commodity will appear on the books as a credit. That credit can be used as initial margin on future trades, with the same limitations as T-bills.

Margin Call Procedures

Each morning brokers will receive a computer printout that lists accounts on margin call. The branch manager is responsible for making sure that the commodity representative handles the calls properly and that the customer meets them. The representative must call the customer for funds, either the day the trade is initiated (if the broker knows additional funds will be required) or the following morning when the call is received.

If the commodity representative is not going to be in the office on a particular day, the branch manager must assign someone else to make the margin calls. When the customer is advised of the call, he or she should let the branch office know how the call will be met.

- If the customer meets the call by liquidating positions, the commodity representative should immediately obtain workable orders from the customer so that the liquidation may take place the day the call is made.
- When funds are to be transferred from another account, the commodity representative should do so immediately.
- If the customer intends to satisfy the call by depositing cash, he or she must immediately put a check in the mail or otherwise arrange for prompt delivery of the check.
- If a customer plans to be out of town, he or she should make arrangements for local payment of margin calls.

New Account Procedure

The following rules apply to the opening of all commodity accounts:

- Accounts will be opened only when the branch manager has in hand all relevant documents and the initial margin deposit.
- To obtain an account number, the branch must provide the customer's name, the commodity representative's number, and confirmation that all new account documents and funds are in hand.
- The branch manager should send all account papers to the headquarters of the FCM promptly after opening an account.
- An initial deposit equal to or greater than $5,000 or the initial margin requirement of the trade must be received before the account begins trading.

Overdue Calls and Sellout Procedures

Commodity representatives are notified on the first day that any of their accounts are on call and each day thereafter. They are expected to contact customers the same day the call is received.

If an account is still on call at 2:00 P.M. on the third day, it is considered overdue. If by noon on the fourth day the margin obligation has not been discharged in an acceptable manner, a Western Union wire will be sent to the customer advising that positions may be liquidated unless the necessary funds are received by a specific time the following day. Subsequent liquidation will be made at the discretion of the branch manager, based on the current status of the account, market conditions, and the customer's past credit standing. Fourth day procedure will be accelerated to the first or second day if any account is in deficit or in imminent danger of going into deficit.

The courts have ruled that customers who knowingly enter positions undermargined are in violation of the Commodity Futures Trading Act. Future commission merchants not only have the right to liquidate positions to protect themselves, but also have a duty to comply with the act and to protect the integrity of the markets.

Customers who bring suit against FCMs frequently use as a defense the lack of action by the FCM to close positions to stop further losses. Many commodity representatives feel that they must accept customer orders, but this is not true. In the first place, if a customer asks a broker to execute an order without sufficient funds to cover initial margins, both of them can be in violation of established rules. In the second place, it is an established rule that brokers must know their customers. Some customers do not have the experience, the expertise, or the funds to make certain trades. The commodity representative is the first person liable for a customer's lack of financial responsibility. Some trades involve so much risk that only large accounts should trade them.

Day Trade

A day trade is one in which the same commodity, same quantity, and same month are bought and sold in the same trading session. An account wishing to day trade must meet the initial margin before establishing the position and be fully margined on other positions. Day trading in accounts that have a deficit or are on call is strictly prohibited. Any commodity representative who does so is subject to suspension from further trading in commodities.

Margin Call Procedures during Delivery Month

The following policy has been established because of the risk involved in trading delivery month contracts:

- Prior to the first notice day, all longs will be called for the entire contract value.
- In the case of shorts, accounts making delivery must have full contract value or warehouse receipts in the broker's hands five days before the contracts expire.

Commodity Order Writing

Commodity representatives should be familiar with correct order procedures. This will avoid costly errors and save valuable time in order entry and execution. Branch managers should pay particular attention to the procedures outlined in this section.

Time-Stamping Order Tickets

The CFTC requires rigid adherence to rules concerning time-stamping of orders. Customer orders must be time-stamped upon receipt. If the commodity representative enters the order, he must time-stamp it a second time when it is transmitted to the order desk. This applies to all orders, whether received during or after market hours. The order ticket must be immediately time-stamped a third time upon receipt of the execution price. It is the commodity representative's responsibility to ensure that orders received from customers are transmitted in the order established by time-stamping. From time to time, the branch manager should review the office's order tickets to be sure brokers are adhering to CFTC regulations concerning time-stamping.

Customer and House Orders

The CFTC requires that customer orders be processed before house orders. This can be verified by time-stamping.

Rules Governing Types of Orders and Order Entry

The following rules govern the types of orders that are acceptable and the procedures for entering these orders:

- All orders are considered day orders unless specified open (GTC). (The Chicago Board of Trade does not accept open orders.)
- If an order is open, the word "open" should be placed before buy or sell.
- If an error is made on an order entered on an outside phone, it will be considered a branch error.

- When entering spread or straddle orders, start with the order on the buy side and specify whether the spread should be done at the market or at a specific difference.

- The Chicago Board of Trade does not accept contingency orders, but the Chicago Mercantile Exchange and most other exchanges do. Be sure to check with specific exchanges.

- Grains are traded in quantities of 5s, or 5,000 bushels. One contract of December corn should be specified as 5 Dec. corn except on the MidAmerica, where the quantity is the number of contracts; i.e., one mid Dec. corn = 1 contract. Quantities on all other exchanges are specified in contracts.

- The minimum fluctuation in grains is 1/4 cent. All other commodities have a minimum of 1 to 10 points.

- When entering orders for commodities traded on more than one exchange, such as gold and silver, it is imperative that the exchange be specified. Gold prices should contain five digits, and silver prices should contain six.

- The designation "OB" (or better) must be used on limit orders to buy and sell when the limit price is close to the current market quote, whether the limit price is above or below the current price.

- Sell stop orders are entered below the market, and buy stop orders are entered above the market.

- Buy MIT orders are entered below the market, and sell MIT orders are entered above the market.

- Straight stop orders in orange juice are unacceptable. All orders entered for this market must be stop limit orders, with the same stop and limit.

- Stop limit orders in cotton must have the same stop and limit prices.

- OCO orders (one cancels the other) are generally unacceptable. Some exchanges do accept them, usually only when the market is slow, but the Chicago Board of Trade does not.

- Stop close only orders are not accepted on the Chicago Board of Trade but are accepted on all other exchanges.

- Stop spread orders are unacceptable.

- All cancellations must include the original order number and order details (if open being canceled, so state).

- When making a change in an order over the hotline, specify whether the original order is a phone or wire order.

- The commodity exchanges will not accept a buy order canceling a sell or a sell order canceling a buy. The cancelation and new order must be treated and entered as two separate orders.
- There is no limit on the number of cancellations which may be entered on an order.
- Orders specifying a commodity month will always be executed for that month of the nearest year. Orders for other than the nearest calendar year must designate the year.
- All orders placed for a floor broker's discretion must carry the designation "not held" (or DRT = Disregard Tape).
- Any order entered within five minutes of the opening of the market is accepted solely at the customer's risk. The floor broker is not held. The Chicago Board of Trade requires 15 minutes.
- Opening only and closing only limit orders are on a "not held" basis.
- Within five minutes of the close of any market, orders to cancel or change a previously entered order are accepted only at the customer's risk because the order may not be filled or an error may be made through failure to cancel the previous order. These orders are accepted on a "not held" basis at the Chicago Board of Trade 15 minutes before the close.
- Never send duplicate orders if you think the order did not get to the right place or was not sent.
- All orders entered wrong will be sent back to the branch, and new orders must be resent.
- Be sure that the price on your order is within the daily range.

Confirmation of Executed Orders

The same day an order is executed, the bookkeeping computer will send written confirmation. Commodity representatives must check the hard copy against their tickets to be sure that both read the same. Additionally, the branch manager must see that the fill is correct. If a branch manager accepts a hard copy that is in error, the error rests with the branch.

If what appears to be an error is detected by comparison of the hard copy and the broker's ticket (i.e., one says buy and one says sell), the broker should immediately call the computer operator and report this discrepancy. At that time, it will be determined if there is an error and where the responsibility lies. The hard copy should be attached to the broker's ticket and retained as a permanent record.

Unreported Executed Orders

It is the commodity representative's duty to determine whether an order has been filled. If the computer fails to report a fill or if a fill is reported incorrectly and the commodity representative does not inquire before the market opens the next day, the executed order and resulting consequences are the responsibility of the commodity representative.

PART FOUR

MONEY MANAGEMENT HANDBOOK

Introduction

The key to success in commodity futures trading is the manner in which the position is handled. In fact, the profits obtained from commodity trading are usually a result of disciplined money management rather than esoteric analysis tools or trading techniques.

Part Four of the text presents practical strategies for position management.

9

THINKING
LIKE A
TRADER

Understanding Hope and Fear

Position management entails not only knowing the rules but following them—even when they contradict emotions. If they are not understood and controlled, the emotions created by market price movement can ruin even an experienced trader.

Traders are often betrayed by hope when the market turns against them. They hope that the price will turn in their favor. The more the price goes against them, the stronger their hope. Eventually hope becomes despair and they exit the market with a huge loss. If the price goes in their favor, fear that the trend will reverse causes them to abandon their position before it develops to fruition. Interestingly, the fear that cuts profits short is often strongest after traders have incurred considerable losses by allowing hope to carry them to despair.

Figure 9.1 indicates how damaging fear and hope, if misused, can be to a commodity trading account.

Figure 9.1

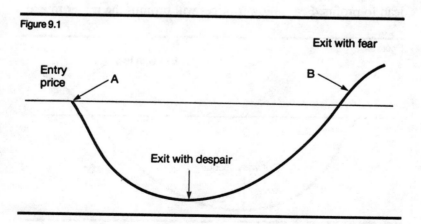

The wavy line represents market action. Markets do not travel in straight lines but undulate as they work to higher or lower prices. This rise and fall influences the trader's emotions and will affect profits if the individual is not well disciplined.

The horizontal line represents the entry level, or the price at which the trade is established. If the trader enters at price *A*, hope keeps him in the market until it dips dramatically; he then exits with despair at nearly the low. If the trader enters the market at point *B* and is overcome by fear, he will exit early and gain only a small profit. In this case, the point of entry is at the middle of the price action. At this point, the trader with misplaced emotions will most certainly lose money.

Admittedly, if the trader is 100 percent accurate in his analysis of price direction, fear and hope make little difference. However, it is unlikely that one will be right in the commodities market 100 percent of the time.

Notice in Figure 9.2 that the entry level to produce a breakeven situation needs to be halfway between the major point of despair and the most likely market exit point. This is at the lower one-third point of the price range. Therefore, the trader must analyze price action accurately 66 percent of the time to break even.

It is important to fear that market action will cause a loss while hoping only when profits are in one's favor. Hoping for higher prices after making a profit will keep one in the market as long as more profits are available. If the market takes an unfavorable turn, fear of mounting losses will drive the trader out in time to avoid a downward spiral.

Figure 9.3 indicates how proper placement of emotions can lead to profits. Fear of lower prices will prompt the trader to exit

Figure 9.2

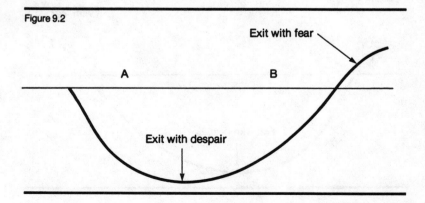

Figure 9.3

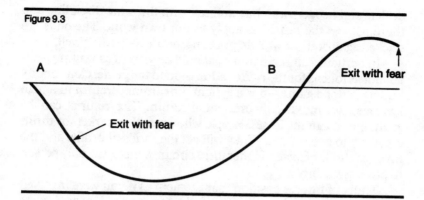

early with a small loss. Hope will lead to large profits by keeping the trader in the market until lower prices seem imminent.

For purposes of illustration, this discussion has focused on the buy side. To gauge the impact of fear and hope on commodity trading in the short position, simply turn the charts upside down, placing hope above the line and fear below it.

No matter how you view it, these emotions can be costly in the commodity marketplace because they impair one's ability to look clearly at price action. The successful trader learns to control hope and fear.

Trading Attitude Survey

Your reactions in the market are likely to parallel your reactions in other situations, so self-knowledge is important. Do you understand what motivates your decisions? Can you predict how you will respond in a given situation? Before proceeding in this chapter, take time out to complete the Trading Attitude Survey in Appendix D. Note that there are no right or wrong answers; each response reveals something about you and your decision-making behavior. Consult the interpretations that follow the survey to find out what your answers mean in terms of your trading potential. If emotions appear to be dominating your behavior, you must begin to develop a more reasoned approach to commodity trading.

Getting Down to Business

The successful investor views speculation as a business activity. More than half the participants in futures markets are professional dealers and hedgers who buy and sell with the same discipline and thoroughness the rest of us apply to our own work. The odds are stacked against those who do not concentrate on trading well.

In particular, margin money should be viewed as venture capital, not as tokens for the ride or admission to the game. Commodity trading is not a game—it is a system for earning a return in a high leverage, fast-moving investment medium. The returns can be great, but so can the losses. People who enter the market for thrills are likely to get just that: They will get the thrills of profits and the inverted thrills of losses. Under these circumstances, the only person to profit is the broker.

Think of futures position management as if you were involved in the business that uses or produces the commodity you are buying or selling on the futures market. Often, the best trader is a person who once was, or still is, involved in the cash item. In fact, many successful futures traders find themselves branching out into the cash side as a natural adjunct to their success in the futures market.

Still, success does not come easily. Some maintain that the farmer who trades soybeans well or the scrap metal dealer who has a handle on metal futures has inside information. More likely, they have the confidence that comes from market feel and a businesslike approach to this trading capital.

To develop a businesslike attitude in your trading, try to imitate the dealer in the cash equivalent of futures. Here are some basic points distilled from the cash trader:

Don't Try to Shoot the Leaves off the Trees

Cash market participants are professional inventory managers in the market for the long haul. They use the futures markets at times of greatest risk. They are less likely to use futures during periods of price stability.

Hedgers will short the market when prices are most likely to decline and go long as prices move out of major lows. They do this knowing that the probability of picking the tops or bottoms is remote. Their cash position allows them to hold their futures positions in strong hands. Knowing that cash gains offset futures losses, their bankers will back this stance.

Buying Is Building

If you believe that buying is building, the building should be done during a time of low-cost resources. Prices, of course, are relative, so it is wise to take the time to determine relative values.

The value of a commodity should relate to historical values, to its substitutes, and to its sensitivity to various economic weather vanes such as gold, interest rates, and foreign exchange rates. Many venture capitalists wait for recessions to expand and build, when no one else has the liquidity to buy. As the saying goes, "Wait for winter to buy your straw hat."

Selling Is Liquidating

A few simple questions can save many dollars in losses. Before shorting or selling a market, ask yourself: "If I didn't own it, would I buy it at this price level? If I owned it, would I sell it at this level?"

Always remember that selling and price declines feed on each other. As price decays, sellers panic and overstay the market, finally throwing off their inventory at distressed prices. Good inventory managers prefer to sell too soon and not squeeze that last nickel from the quote machine. Although hard to set in practice, sales into a top-heavy market are possible with substantial margin and disciplined stops. As a rule, price declines are rapid and fit well into the short-term trading strategy. This reflects the seven months up and two-to-three months down pattern of most composite commodity indexes.

Buy Dips and Sell Rallies

This is one of the oldest and most difficult trading principles to set in motion.

Put yourself in the position of the cash market dealer. If you want to build material inventories, isn't it best to do so during price pullbacks, when the product is available and price is liquid? If you are trying to liquidate inventory, shouldn't you do so during price rallies? Some people describe the activity of buying dips as a contrarian technique—contrary to the minor trend but confident in the major trend. You are dealing in the long term—the tides of price—not the eddies and whirlpools of short-term fluctuation.

A logical approach, tempered with money management to protect against a bad forecast, puts you in the same league with a Cargill grain dealer, a Hershey's cocoa buyer, or a silver trader for the Bank of Mexico.

Put All Your Eggs in One Basket

This axiom flies in the face of typical investment thinking, but there is a logic to it. For instance, consider an entrepreneur with a variety of businesses. As those ventures mature, the owner will add capital to the most profitable and sell off the losers. The level of capital commitment reflects his or her confidence in the profit potential of the venture.

As you trade commodities, be willing to put the most money into the high potential trades. Concentrate on the winners.

Take a Vacation Once in a While

It is wise to take a vacation from the markets. Reward yourself when you do well. When you do badly, take a breather. If you need help in pulling away, join T.A.—Traders Anonymous. The market and its profit opportunities will always be there. Certain periods have little to offer, so don't convince yourself that you must be in the market every day.

Money Management Setup Rules

Many commodity traders have entered positions in which they were ultimately right but, due to the lack of position management, were under-margined. They were wiped out by price fluctuation before the profit of the trade could be realized. Consider the following money management techniques when establishing a position:

Establish a Goal

As you establish your trading goals, gather as much input as you can. Consider how much time you will devote to your commodity trading and what percent of your investment portfolio you will devote to trading in commodity futures. The watchword is realism. Be realistic with your trading goals, but be sure to put an actual dollar value on them.

Start Small

If you haven't traded in the past, it is best to start small until you become more comfortable with the technique. Initial positions in the market should be smaller than the positions you will eventually scale into.

Follow the Major Trend

Many of the great businesspeople of our era have been follow-ers, not leaders. They give the markets what they want and profit from them. They let the market commit itself first, then climb on board. The longer the trend, the more comfortable the market position should be.

Know the Tax Benefits

The tax character of trading is very individual. Look closely at its advantages to your particular situation.

Set Your Own Margin Level

It is important to remember that the margins prescribed by brokers and exchanges are their money management techniques, not yours. Margins are designed to protect the integrity of the market. They may not protect your integrity or potential profits, so you must determine your own margin level. Your personal requirements may be greater.

Separate Short- and Long-Term Thinking

Avoid letting the short-term chop of the market affect your long-term thinking. Keep in mind that a major bull move will have several dips before reaching its peak. Don't let short-term bearish market action deprive you of your profits.

Start a Trading Diary

One of the best ways to manage commodity positions is by keeping a diary (see sample on following page). As you enter the market, write down your reasons for making the trade—not only the market factors, but your personal motives. Include both your profit objective and your bailout point. If you can't formulate good, solid reasons for being involved in a trade, you shouldn't be in it. Figure your risk-reward ratio by dividing the objective by the amount of loss allowed. If the objective is for 12 points profit and the stop loss is placed 4 points from the entry point, divide 12 by 4. The risk-reward ratio would be 1:3.

Selecting the Amount of Money to Trade

Selecting the appropriate amount of money to place in the trading account reduces the influence of emotions while providing an adequate capital to make an impact on one's net worth if the trading is profitable.

Often, beginning traders use too large a portion of their invest-

TRADING DIARY PAGE

Date _____

Are commodities as a group in an uptrend or downtrend?

What analysis tool was used to determine market trend?

What is the trend of the individual commodity groups?

Grains:

Meats:

Metals:

Financials:

Food/Fiber:

What are the best trades?

Commodity	Prefer Entry Point	Stop Loss	Price Objective	Risk/Reward Ratio	Reason for Trace

ment capital in commodity trading. Confident that they can control their emotions and that they will be right and profitable in their trading, they put a disproportionate amount of money in their trading account.

Too little of one's investment capital can also be a problem. If only 5 percent of an individual's risk capital is placed in commodities and trading is able to double that amount, the impact on one's investment funds would only be 5 percent.

There are a number of formulas for selecting the proper risk capital that should be devoted to commodities. The following formula has proven to be as good as most.

First, determine the prospective trader's total net worth. The investment capital should be at least 10 percent of the total net worth. Of course, as an individual's net worth increases, the investment capital is usually proportionately greater. Once the investment capital has been determined, use no less than 10 percent and no more than 2 percent of that capital in a high risk situation.

For example, if an individual has a net worth of $500,000 the amount of investment capital will probably be more than 10 percent, or $50,000+. The amount of money to be placed in a risk-bearing account would then be $10,000 or less. This is the smallest investment any one would justifiably recommend to a beginning commodity trader.

Some informal studies have indicated that the larger the amount of investment capital placed in commodity trading, the greater the chance for success. The rough percentages are as follows:

- With $5,000 in a commodity trading account, the probability for success after one year is 1 out of 10.
- With $10,000 in a commodity trading account, the probability for success after one year is 2 out of 10.
- With $20,000 in a commodity trading account, the probability for success after one year is 3 out of 10.
- With $50,000 in a commodity trading account, the probability for success after one year is 5 out of 10.
- With $100,000 in a commodity trading account, the probability for success after one year is 6 out of 10.

Notice that the odds are stacked against the trader with less than $50,000 in an individual commodity trading account. This certainly heightens the importance of good money management techniques.

10

POSITION MANAGEMENT STRATEGIES

Paper Trading

The only accurate way to document performance is to keep a diary—a log of trading activities. For the beginning trader, this is a prerequisite and a companion activity to implementing the money management techniques found herein.

A few years ago, the Chicago Mercantile Exchange (CME) created a format for beginning traders to use to test their paper trading skills. It is called the *Commodities Scorecard* and is still available by writing to the CME. This format can be used by the beginning trader to document market entry and exit prices and to calculate profit and loss. Accompanying the format are rules for determining what prices for entry and exit could be considered valid, although hypothetical.

For instance, if the trader specifies a purchase of a commodity on a particular day and then a later sale of that commodity, it's not valid to use the low of the day as the purchase price and the high of the day as the price of the sale. Due to the effects of emotion in commodity trading, it would be more realistic to choose the high of the day as the purchase price and the low of the day as the sell price.

Paper trading is the first step to understanding commodity trading but should not be misconstrued as a valid test of one's ability to make money. The greatest value in paper trading is not the knowledge that you are right or wrong, but the discipline gained by watching price action.

Use the form on the following page to record your paper trading. (Use the table at the end of Chapter 5 to help figure profits and losses from your paper trading.)

Price Charting

An activity similar to paper trading is price charting—recording the daily price movement of several commodities. (Incidentally, price

Paper Trading

No. of Contracts	Commodity	Buy Price	Sell Price	Strategy for Making Trade	Profit (Loss)

charting and chart analysis are not necessarily concurrent activities.) Charting helps one discover the character of price movement, a far more important activity than the sterile observation of technical formations.

The first steps in commodity trading are knowing what you want to do and knowing what the market is doing. Keeping a log of trading activities while charting market activity is a beginning to the fulfillment of these two objectives.

If you are beyond these two stages, you can move ahead to the other position management procedures described in this chapter.

The Trend

The trend must be concurrent with the direction of your position for at least the duration of your position if you are to make profits as a commodity trader. Perhaps it seems basic and unsophisticated to ride the trend rather than to select turning points and reversals or aberrations and departures. Sophisticated market analysis techniques are not inappropriate, but they will be ineffectual without an acknowledgment of trend.

We sometimes find ourselves bargain hunting in the commodity markets. We hear ourselves saying, "The price has gone down so long it must be about ready to go up," or "The price has risen to historical highs, so it probably won't go much higher."That's when we get into trouble. The extreme of price movement in either direction does not necessarily correlate with a propensity of the market to reverse.

Determining Trend

To determine the trend, start by looking at the market. Will Rogers, who is not particularly known for his ability to invest profitably, once quipped, "The best way to make money in the stock market is to buy something that is going up. If it doesn't go up, don't buy it." It is easy to determine the past trend, but predicting whether it will continue is more difficult. It is best not to ask how long the trend will last, but what will signal its end.

This is where hope and fear defy us once again. If we buy something that is trending higher and the price begins to fall soon after the purchase, we hope that the trend will renew. A better placed emotion is fear. If we buy something and the price moves against us, it is best to fear that the trend will change. This will keep us alert and flexible enough to abandon the position before losses are devastating.

As you enter a position, determine at what point you will be convinced that the trend has changed, and be prepared to bail out at that point. This technique will teach you to admit when you are wrong, which is an important lesson to learn. You will be wrong more often than right as you trade commodities.

Three-Unit Trading Technique For Short-Term Positions

As you enter short-term positions, consider using the three-unit trading technique. Commissions are a large component in short-term trading, but this technique pays the fare early in the trade. Here's how it works:

1. Enter the market with a number of contracts divisible by three.
2. Take profits on one of the three units after the market has moved enough to pay the commissions on all three. For example, if the commission for soybeans is $50 per contract, then a move of 3 cents wil pay commissions on all three units.
3. Take profits on a second unit after the market has met its initial objective.
4. Let the third unit run and exit as you are convinced of a top or bottom.

Use the three-unit trading technique only in situations with a 1:3 or better risk-to-reward ratio. If the market moves against you to the full risk objective, get out of all three units.

Protecting and Multiplying Profits

Once the market begins to move in his favor, the trader must try to protect and multiply his profits.

Protective stops cut both ways—they prevent big losses but also can curb long-term profits. The trader needs a system of placing protective stops that can protect profits without needlessly being stopped out of the market during a minor retracement. Stops should be established on the basis of logic. Although there are numerous ways to calculate the placement of stops, all protective stops fall into two general categories—market following stops and market reversal stops.

Market Following Stops

Market following stops lag the market by a calculable distance. They are generally a short-term trading technique, often used to take windfall profits, to protect the profits, or to prevent losses of short-term trades. Placement of the market following stop can be as subjective as the trader's opinion or it can be calculated. The following technique is an effective way to calculate the placement of a market following stop.

Once paper profits have been generated and an uptrend or downtrend has been established, determine the daily range of that commodity's price. Measure the amount between each day's high and low.

After determining the range of trading for each of the days contained within the trend, calculate the weighted average for the range for the last 10 days. This weighted average will tell you the volume of "noise" the market is creating each day on an average, with the greatest importance placed on the most recent market activity.

To calculate a weighted average, arrange the numbers to be averaged in chronological order, the most recent number last.

Multiply the oldest number by 1, the next by 2, the next by 3 and so on, until you reach the most recent number which will be multiplied by a factor that is the total number of entries. If you are averaging five numbers, the most recent number will be multiplied by 5.

Then, add all the results and divide by the sum of the multipliers. This will give you the weighted average.

The following is a weighted average calculation for values of five daily ranges:

Day 1	Day 2	Day 3	Day 4	Day 5
7	8	7	10	11

$$\frac{(1 \times 7) + (2 \times 8) + (3 \times 7) + (4 \times 10) + (5 \times 11)}{(1 + 2 + 3 + 4 + 5)}$$

$$\frac{(7 + 16 + 21 + 40 + 55)}{15} = 9.3$$

Notice that the weighted average (9.3) is greater than a simple average (8.6) because greater emphasis is placed on the most recent values.

To avoid being stopped out by the market's noise, you must place your stops beyond the range of that noise.

Think of the daily trading range of the market as a psychological tide. Each day the market sets its high and ebb tide mark. As the psychology of the market evolves and the trend matures, the distance between the high tide mark and the low tide mark normally becomes greater if the trend is up, less if the trend is down. The weighted average is used to give the most credibility to the most recent prices.

Now that you have the weighted average, application is straightforward. Multiply the weighted average times 1.5. If the weighted average were 2 points, your stop placement would use the number 3.

To use this number to place the stop on Wednesday, use Tuesday's trading range. If you are protecting profits in a short position, determine the middle of Tuesday's range and add the factored weighted average to the price that represents the middle of Tuesday's range. Subtract the factored weighted average value if you are protecting profits from a long position. This technique will allow the market to make the noise of its daily price-making activity but will only take you out of the market if it exceeds its normal psychological benchmarks.

Another commonly used technique for stop placement is less mathematical but serves the same purpose as the factored weighted average approach. Many traders simply place their stop just below a low of the second preceding day in an uptrend or below the high of the second preceding day in a downtrend. In other words, to protect profits in a long position, the stop you place on Thursday should be just below the low on Tuesday.

Stops at Market Reversals

Certainly the most common type of protective stop is at points of expected market reversal. Because of its popularity, the reversal protective stop can be self-defeating. If the location of the stop is logical, it will probably be apparent to many people, so special cautions should be observed.

The More Obvious the Reversal Point, the More Stops Will Be Placed at That Point

Breaks in trendlines, key reversals, and head and shoulder reversals are technical reversal formations that are used to determine a specific stop placement. When placing stops in regard to these formations, keep in mind that you are placing the stop in a crowd and that the fill of your stop order may be near limit from the previous day's close.

After Reversal, Observe Market Activity

After the reversal has been recorded, market activity will reveal whether it is possible to get out of the market with a better than limit up or limit down fill. This is particularly helpful if you are keeping a mental stop or if you are considering placing a stop after a reversal formation.

If the market slams limit down after making a reversal top and does not trade at the limit position, the market is likely to offer little help for your cause. But if the market moves to limit down, then trades actively at that position, long positions are being created. These long positions may be generating support to offer some price relief within which you can exit the market.

Many Markets Give You a Second Chance

Many technicians refer to the pullback effect after a reversal formation. As trendlines are broken, there is a propensity for the market to retrace back to the price of the breakout before further decline. The commodity's price history will reveal whether or not this holds true.

In recent years, the soybean market has been known to give the trader a second chance to get out. Not taking that second chance can impair your financial condition. Study the price history of a commodity and see the devastation caused by ignoring this pullback effect.

Consider Using Orders Other Than Stops for Market Exit

The stop limit order is often effective when placed in a crowd of stop orders. On first blush, it resembles the garden variety stop.

A stop limit order to buy is placed in the same location relative to the existing market price as a buy stop. A sell top limit is placed in the same location relative to the existing market as a sell stop. The results, however, differ.

The effect of the stop limit order is that after the stop price is activated, the order is filled as a limit order rather than a market order as in a normal stop. You have a "second chute" protection. Look at an example of a stop limit in action.

If the Treasury bill market is trading at 91.00 and a move to 90.00 would break the uptrend line, you may want to place a sell stop limit at 90.00. A price move from 91.00 would activate the stop, but the stop limit order dictates that you must be filled at 90.00 or better. If the execution of stop orders were to accelerate the price through 90.00 and the activity of traders evening up were to bring the price back to 90.00 or above, your order would be executed at a preferred price. You have a better chance of exiting after the washout than during it.

Another important consideration of the stop limit order is that the stop price and the limit price need not be at the same price level. For example, if the current market price for T-bills is 91.00 and a trendline would be broken on a move to 90.00, you could place an order at 90.00 stop, 89.75 limit. This would give the market a 25-point latitude to fill your order, and you would be filled at 89.75 or better.

Avoid Using the "Cancel if Close" (CIC) Order

This is a fictitious order for a real phenomenon. Many novice traders lose confidence in their stop placement and carry with them a mental order to pull the stop, coined the "cancel if close" order. If you had a good reason to place a stop at a particular location, your reason for canceling that stop must be even better.

One of the most important considerations of commodity position management is when and if to pyramid paper profits. Many great traders suggest that the only way to build major profits is to pyramid as your account equity provides enough profits to margin additional positions. Remember though, "Dead pharaohs lie under many great pyramids."

Using Stops in a Pyramid

Pyramiding in regard to the long-term strategy should carry with it some special considerations.

Suppose that you have a position that is three months old and that the option in which you have long position profits does not expire for several months. If you are seeking long-term capital gains, first decide whether to pyramid in the option in which you already have profits or to seek long-term capital gains on the pyramided position.

If your aim is long-term gains, select a contract with an expiration of at least six months and one day from the present date. When placing your stop in a pyramided position, decide whether you will protect the entire position or just your initial position. If you are protecting the entire position, your stop may destroy your chances for long-term capital gains.

Handle a pyramided position as a group of different trades. For each additional position, review the existing risk-reward ratios, market entry techniques, and stop placement. You cannot be less careful in building a pyramid than you were in establishing its foundation. Profits can make you forget to discipline your trading—a fatal flaw. You earned those profits by taking a risk. Learn how to keep them.

Following are key considerations in pyramiding.

Pyramid Only at Points Where You Would Initiate a Position if You Didn't Already Have One

Before you pyramid a position, ask yourself, "If I didn't already have a position in this market, would I establish one here?"

Pyramid at Particular Buy Signals or Sell Signals

Whatever technique you use to determine buy or sell levels should be used to dictate when you pyramid in existing profitable positions. If you are a technical trader and feel comfortable buying breakouts of flags and pennants or retracements, these should be the times to consider pyramiding.

Establish a New Margin Level

If your initial position was margined with $10,000 margin, do not pyramid until you have $10,000 additional equity in your account. At that point, pyramid with one-half or less of your original contracts. This helps you to avoid the greatest peril of pyramiding—creating an average price that is too high. If you pyramid with only one-half the number of contracts of your original position, your price average level will be only one-third higher than your original price level.

Anatomy of a Bull Market

Major bull markets have characteristic anatomies that should be dissected historically to determine the peculiarities of a future rally. Early acknowledgment of the similar characteristics of a major bull market gives us the opportunity for major profit at very low risk with very high potentials.

The foundations for a major bull market can be observed with fundamental as well as technical analysis if the trader has enough patience to discover the elusive benchmarks.

The anatomy we offer here will describe the bull market in both fundamental and technical terms. This is not to deny the existence of cyclical, seasonal, and other analysis benchmarks, for they, too, can give early signals of these highly profitable markets.

Stage One—The Birth of the Bull

Surprisingly, the origins of a bull market are found in surplus situations. High prices in a bull market usually develop in times of shortages, but surplus supplies actually set the stage for an explosive rally. Surplus commodities widen the arteries, fill the pipelines, and foster new sources of demand—and the demand characteristic is often an inelastic one. An industry whose raw materials are in surplus is likely to expand. Surplus supplies build confidence in the user—the confidence to expand, to solicit new customers, and to contract long-term commitments. All of these factors result in an increased appetite and a wide demand base.

Technically, a surplus market is observable as a rounded bottom, the early signs of which are progressively shallowing downtrends and narrower trading ranges. Many major bull markets begin as a rounded bottom technical formation. The absolute bottom of a rounded bottom often occurs when the fundamental information is the most bearish while the commodity price meanders sideways in a narrow range. You can be comfortable with a major market bottom when all the news reports say that corn is going to the price of gravel while the corn price wanders aimlessly in a 2-cent range. Passive market activity under bearish news is your first bull sign.

Stage Two—Shallow Uptrend

The next benchmark to look for is modestly increasing prices, exhibited as the right side of the rounded bottom—a very shallow uptrend. This is often accompanied by wider price ranges.

Fundamentally, there is little change in the supply of the commodity, although commercial interest in the commodity changes slightly. A "what if" stage develops among the fundamentalists; e.g., What if there is a short wheat crop in Russia? What if Brazilian coffee has a freeze? What if housing starts increase by 10 percent? Due to the intangible nature of the "what if" stage and the fruitless nature of most "what if" scenarios, stage two offers very little price improvement other than the gradual increase in price due to carrying charges.

Stage Three—The Breakout

The third stage of development of a major bull market is a very interesting one that often occurs with very little public fundamental information. It is often described in business publications as a technical breakout, which is a way of saying, "The market has made a dramatic move but we don't know why."

Technically, the market is breaking out of the rounded bottom, and it usually shows a modest rally for a few days, sometimes weeks. This rally often subsides without fundamental follow-through, and the market develops what is technically termed a platform. This is sideways market activity at the area of the rounded bottom breakout and is a time of confusing information. Fundamental and technical data during this time period are often conflicting, and market information is often contradictory.

Stage Four—The Rally Begins

Stage four of the bull market develops as market information becomes more detailed. Often, seemingly minor fundamental information comes into play, such as erratic weather patterns across the Midwest affecting the grain market. "What if" scenarios also begin to develop. This is a nervous rally—it tends to be choppy with labored price increases and sharp, quick dips. The rallies and subsequent dips are usually able to hold a 45-degree trendline, and the trader can feel confident in buying the dips back to the trendline.

Stage Five—The Explosive Newsmaker

Technically, gaps are left on the charts during this time, and the bullish fundamental scenario enjoys wider acceptance. Users are often scrambling to purchase raw material, while sellers become more reluctant. Interestingly, newsletters during this stage often become nervous and indicate a bias that the market may be topping.

Stage Six—The Steep Rally

The sixth stage of the bull market is typically a steep rally with few market retracements and wide trading ranges fueled by bullish fundamental information. Often, public attention will turn toward the market rally and people who have never traded commodities will suddenly think about buying.

During this period, the media report news of users who are going bankrupt because they have left themselves exposed to price increases in dramatic raw materials.

Stage Seven—The Shearing

Stage seven occurs when investors decide to sell their blue chip stock at a loss and go long in the commodity. This is when bullish information is being offered to the public and the public is inspired to become involved. Technically, the market will gap higher with limit up moves, even for two or more days; then the sheep are shorn. It is after stage seven that the industry is plagued with outcries for greater regulation.

W. D. Gann Revised

W. D. Gann is one of history's most noted Wall Street successes. During his commodity and stock trading years in the early part of this century, he amassed tens of millions of dollars while documenting his trading techniques in a market newsletter and numerous books.

He summarized his money management techniques for stock trading into 24 rules. In the following pages, I have revised these 24 rules to be applicable to commodity trading.

1. *Determine the Proper Amount of Capital to Use*
   Divide the amount of risk capital that you are devoting to the commodities markets into ten equal parts and never risk more than one-tenth of this risk capital on any one trade.

2. *Use Stop Loss Orders*
   Always protect a trade with a protective stop that is determined by using risk-reward ratios and the stop placement techniques mentioned earlier.

3. *Never Overtrade*
   One often makes this mistake after reaping a considerable profit from a recent trade. Confidence will have built up and the trader will make the mistake of entering the market with a larger than usual position. Overtrading also occurs when a trader tries to recoup losses.

4. *Never Let a Profit Run into a Loss*
   Once you have a profit, raise your stop loss order so that you will have no loss of capital on the trade.

5. *Never Buck the Trend*
   It is particularly important to know the trend of the market before you buy or sell.

6. *If You Don't Know Why You Are in a Trade or Are Not Confident of the Market's Direction, It Is Best to Abandon Your Position.*
   Never enter a trade when you are in doubt.

7. *Trade Only Liquid Markets*
   Those are the active commodities traded. There are plenty of good, viable commodity markets offering profit without going into left field and trying to trade the markets that are thinly traded and dominated by commercial or local interests.

8. *Try to Diversify Your Risk*
   Trade commodities from various groupings to balance your account. Try to avoid tying up all your trading capital in one commodity or commodity grouping.

9. *Trade Only with Market Orders*
   Fixing a buying or selling price can be dangerous and should only be used when you have a specific purpose in entering a limited price on your order.

10. *Don't Close Out Your Trades Unless You Have Good Reason*
    Following the trade with a stop loss order will protect your profits but will not allow you to exit the market on a whim. Let the market tell you what should be done. If you are wrong, let the market kick you out.

11. *As You Produce Profits, Place These Profits into a Surplus Account to be Used Only in an Emergency*
    This will help you to avoid becoming egotistical about your commodity trading and will discipline you to stay on the original track that you have set out for yourself.

12. *Never Enter Commodity Trading for Tax Purposes Alone*

13. *Never Average a Loss*
    If you have a loss in the market, do not increase the size of your position to lower your average loss. This is one of the worst mistakes a trader can make.

14. *Do Not Lose Patience in Your Positions*
    Don't exit the market simply because you have lost patience or because you are anxious from waiting.

15. *Avoid Taking Small Profits and Large Losses*

16. *Never Cancel a Stop Loss Order After You Have Placed It*

17. *Avoid Churning Your Account*
    Avoid getting in and out of the market too often. Position your trades and stick with them.

18. *Don't Be a One-Way Trader*
    Be willing to sell short just as often as you are willing to buy. Let your object be to keep with the trend and make a profit.

19. *Don't Buy Because You Think the Commodity Is Oversold or Too Low. Don't Sell Just Because the Price Seems Too High*

20. *It is Dangerous to Pyramid at the Wrong Time*
    The best time to pyramid is when the commodity has broken resistance levels and has become active. Treat a pyramided position as a totally new position. If you would not buy if you didn't already have a position, then you shouldn't be pyramiding the position.

21. *It Is Best to Pyramid on the Buy Side if the Open Interest Has Dipped. It Is Best to Pyramid on the Sell Side After the Open Interest Has Risen*

22. *Never Spread off a Loss*
    If you are in a loss position, get out. Do not spread the position and compound your error.

23. *Never Change Your Position in the Market Without Good Reason*

24. *Avoid Increasing Your Trading after a Long Period of Success or a Period of Profitable Trades*

APPENDIXES

A

FINANCIAL FUTURES INTRODUCTION

Financial futures have produced sophisticated trading and pricing techniques, but the basics of these markets are much easier to understand than one might expect.

Financial or fixed income futures are a child of the times, fostered by the economic climate that developed in the early 1970s. The previous two decades had no use for such a vehicle because debt and inflation rates were still manageable. The 1970s ushered in a period of accelerating commodity inflation, deficit financing, and the monetizing of those deficits. In addition, currencies floated freely to add to the financial chaos. The result of unmanageable money costs is bankruptcy.

Because of restrictions—regulations Q and R—thrift institutions were unable to compete successfully for the saver's dollar as the costs of money rose. Meanwhile, their revenues were restricted by lower rate mortgages. When costs exceed revenues, cash flows dry up and banks either fail or merge.

Other factors besides vertical rate increases and commodity inflation account for the development of financial futures markets. First of all, debt demand swelled in the 1970s. Outstanding debt plus loan guarantees, public and private, may exceed $8.5 trillion—five times more than our Gross National Product. Before the decade was over, inflation rates had reached levels rarely seen in the last two centuries, except in times of war.

The groundrules changed and futures broadened their appeal. New ways to hedge volatility in financial assets and liabilities came into being: foreign currencies, gold, bonds, bills, GNMAs, and, in 1981, certificates of deposits. The inflationary climate drew a new participant into futures—those who were hardest hit by rising prices—the consumer.

Interest rates cut into the consumer's income. For a while, corporations insulated themselves from the gathering financial storm. They fine-tuned their inventory management, passing higher costs along to the consumer.

Financial institutions fared much better than either industrial firms or consumers. How did banks respond? When faced with higher money costs, they simply increased their loan rate. Only those credit users who were naked to the impact of rising interest rates, such as the small borrower and thrift institutions, bled red ink.

Whatever the figure, current debt levels are unmanageably large. Economic historians assessing the last decade may well call it the Decade of Debt. Businesses let their debt increase and capitalized themselves with debt rather than sales. The private sector produced a bumper crop of new land and home mortgages, not to mention corporate bonds. Meanwhile, the federal government permitted enlarged deficits during business expansions.

Responding to inflation and swelling debt loads, investors made millions by leveraging their ownership, weathering reversals, and selling for higher prices after a financial setback.

This hold and dump approach became a way of life for everyone—corporations, investors, and individuals—and it bred cyclically higher interest rates. As interest rates rose, the cost of holding an inventory increased. This in turn caused cash flow problems requiring immediate financing. Like a dog biting its own tail, the debt fed itself.

An increasing debt load feeds on itself and can paralyze private enterprise. The higher the interest rates, the more quickly debt compounds itself. This debt mountain still remains a financial obstacle to a healthy economy. Time will tell whether Reagan's economic policies are successful, but is the federal government truly willing to pay off its debt in more expensive dollars? To do so would fly in the face of the economic behavior of borrowers over the last three decades.

Another factor that nurtured the concept of financial futures is the electronic economy. Money now travels through communication lines as well as in check mailbags on airplanes. If I write a check in California and the bank wants to be sure it clears, it can verify the balance of my account through an electronic checking system. If the check is sufficiently large, it may be worthwhile to check an account balance electronically. In addition, banks are experimenting with consumer banking through home computers.

In general, the computer has given small banks and consumers a more sophisticated means of adapting to changes in interest rates. International financial markets beat with nearly one pulse. For example, Germany's Lombard rate may stimulate an investor in Canada who has Canadian dollars to convert Canadian dollars to Deutsch marks to benefit from the higher interest rate in Germany—all done in a split second by computers, telephone lines, and satellites.

The electronic economy impacts each of us in subtle ways. These supercharged means of funds transfer and investing permit shock waves to move through the world's market with lightning speed. If Morgan Guaranty Bank in New York sets a trend in interest rates and raises its prime by one point, others will follow quietly down the banking chain.

The electronic economy wires the money and currency markets directly into a communications network of telephones, television, and radio. Reaction time is shortened dramatically, uncertainty increases, and adjustments speed up—all producing ever-greater instability. For example, economists attribute to 1980 the shortest recession on record and to 1981 the briefest recovery on record—all within the environment of record rises and plunges in money costs.

On October 6, 1979, Federal Reserve Chairman Paul Volcker changed the groundrules for monetary policy. He enacted credit restraints, laid out a plan to curb growth in money stocks, and let the interest rates seek their own level. He also increased the discount rate by an unprecedented two full points—double the hike of August 1929 which preceded the stock market crash. Not too surprisingly, by February 1980 the bond market had posted losses in the hundreds of billions. The austere measures taken by the Fed sent a shock wave that was felt in a matter of days. Price charts for financial futures such as bonds and GNMAs reveal a widespread destruction of assets.

The implications of the electronic economy are obvious. A major collapse of the financial system is possible in a moment. What took four years, 1929-1933, might break and bottom in months—even weeks—due to electronic communications. Investors can change the complexion of their portfolios more rapidly and with greater leverage.

Financial futures took root and grew in the fertile soil of a spastic economy driven by inflation, debt demand, and electronic communications. Each factor has fostered violent interest rate fluctuation. Quicker reaction time stirs the economic waters and exaggerates price fluctuation of debt instruments.

The growth and character of financial futures were shaped by a factor known as delivery facility. The first interest rate future to be traded was the GNMA (Ginnie Mae), developed by Richard Sandor in 1975. In examining the feasibility of a financial futures market, which had been considered by industry leaders since 1972, Sandor thought a consumer debt instrument would be most popular. Remember, the consumer was hit hardest by interest rate changes. In addition, the Ginnie Mae already enjoyed standardization through the forward markets at mortgage banks and S&Ls. As a result of government regulations, the Ginnie Mae was a relatively homogeneous debt instrument with an active cash market.

Prior to mortgage futures, the Ginnie Mae market as a cash market often lacked liquidity. Moreover, this illiquidity cropped up at critical points—when interest rates were extremely high or low. During stable periods, buyers and sellers were plentiful—a common trait in any market, particularly one that is leveraged.

Just like grain futures a century prior, the futures market in mortgages created a facility for those who wanted to sell their Ginnie Maes and those who wanted to buy them. Investors would go to the market and take long or short positions depending on whether or not they wanted to receive or provide delivery. Shorts provided delivery, and longs accepted delivery.

Debt financing, a common practice in the 1970s, made financial futures a very useful vehicle to manage risk. For example, a corporation knows that it will receive a certain amount of income during a time period and knows that a certain proportion of it will flow into short-term credit instruments, T-bills, commercial paper, or money market funds. If that income is six months away, the cash money markets offer only very limited ways to secure future short-term rates. An investor cannot go to the U.S. government and say, "By the way, I am going to put $5,000 down on this $10,000 T-bill and I will give you the rest a little later." All the money must come up front.

With the advent of futures, money market investors who plan to buy those instruments some time out in the future finally gained a way to price their yield in advance. They can now finance a long or short position on a debt instrument through futures at less than 10 percent of the total value of the contract. With T-bills, the margin commitment is closer to 2 percent. They need only 2 percent to secure an interest rate until it is time to invest the income.

Further changes in banking, savings habits, and debt may change the complexion of financial futures as the markets become more sophisticated and the user's needs change. The 1980s will test new products such as CDs and Eurodollars, both in the U.S. and on exchanges in Canada and England. Other hedging vehicles, such as stock indexes, will also find a place to trade.

The method of pricing financial futures is confusing to some traders, but it needn't be. It's as straightforward as a Series E savings bond. The market prices bonds in two different ways. One method is price, and the other is *percent of par*.

If you decide to buy a $25 Series E bond, offering a premium interest rate of $5\frac{1}{2}$ percent, you will pay only $18.75 for it. The banker will talk to you about price rather than the interest rate or yield on the bond. Over a given period of maturity, your bond will generate a $25 value, or 100 percent of par. The par price refers to the price of the bond at a given yield and maturity.

If the September T-bonds sold yesterday at 63-16, it does not mean that a T-bond yesterday cost $63.16. The par price of a T-bond is 100 percent at 8 percent for 30 years. If the interest rate rises, then this percent of par must decline. Even though the futures quote is not strictly the price, it is a very fair representation of price. The price is $63\frac{16}{32}$ or 63.5 percent of par.

B

COMMODITY OPTIONS VERSUS FUTURES

An ideal investment vehicle is one that offers profit potential at a predetermined risk of loss. If the maximum loss can be calculated before funds are committed, and the profit potential is far greater than the risk, the investment is attractive. If this investment eliminates the need to analyze minor movements and to place protective stops against minor reversals, it is raised one step toward perfection.

Theoretically, one should never purchase a commodity future today unless a major move is about to begin. If the move is not expected to occur for several weeks or months, the sophisticated money manager will hold cash or commit funds to other investments in order to earn a return until the move is underway.

To avoid the risk that the timing is off, or that the anticipated move will not materialize, a stop-loss order should always be entered simultaneously with the commitment. Failure to do so often results in major losses, or even complete loss of invested capital.

Regardless of the number of declines or their severity, complete protection is provided against any and all declines during the life of the option. The problems of timing and the price at which the initial stop-loss order is set, so important to the ultimate success of the commodity futures speculator, can be ignored by the option purchaser.

Both British and American commodity options fit the dictionary definition of option as a right, usually purchased, to buy or sell something at a specified price within a specified time.

When a speculator purchases a commodity option, he or she is purchasing the right to assume a position in the futures at a certain price, called the strike price, and within a certain period of time, running from the purchase date to the declaration date. The option specifies the commodity, the amount or number of contracts, the price at which a futures position is taken if the option is exercised, whether it is an option to take a long or short position in that future, the declaration date on which the option expires, and the premium or charge paid by the buyer to the seller for granting the option.

The premium cost is determined by the time remaining on the option and the volatility of the underlying commodity. The longer the time and the more volatile the commodity, the higher the premium. Trading in options can be done for a period extending to 11 months in optionable commodities, and in some cases for even longer periods. The cost of the premium tends to fluctuate between 5 percent and 15 percent of the striking price. During the life of an option, no original or variation margin calls are made on the buyer (taker).

An option covers only one futures contract. If the owner of an option wishes to take up the futures position, he so notifies the seller of the option and exercises his option. A *put* is an option to enter a short (sell) position; a *call* is an option to enter a long (buy) position; and a *double option* gives the buyer the right to enter either the long or short side, but only one, at the stated price. The cost of a double option is usually twice the amount of an individual call or put option.

Call Option Trading Techniques

Purchase Calls—Anticipating a Price Rise

One of the most basic trading techniques is the purchase of a call in anticipation of a major upward move. Assume that in August 1982, July 1983 sugar is at 6.20. A strong upward move is expected to carry the price to 9.00. The sophisticated futures buyer going long might place a stop at 5.50. An alternative to buying the future for $1,000 margin, risking over $800 if stopped out, would be to pur-

DETAILS OF THE COMMODITY OPTION
Commodity
Basis months and year
Type of option
Number of options
Date purchased
Declaration (expiration) date
Strike price
Premium cost
Commission

chase one six-month call option on July 1983 sugar at a premium cost of $672 with a declaration date of February 9, 1983. Since options are struck at the market price, the call would have a 6.20 strike price. Purchasing this call position means that the buyer (taker) is now potentially long 112,000 pounds of July 1983 sugar at 6.80, calculated by adding the striking price of 6.20 to the premium cost of $672, expressed as .60 in market points. (Dollar premium costs are converted to trading or market points by dividing the dollar premium by the dollar value of one market point.)

The maximum loss to the call buyer is the cost of the premium. The maximum loss will occur only if the option is not exercised or converted because the market does not move above the 6.20 level. On the other hand, if the market does move above the strike price, the size of the loss decreases as the price rises until the break even point is reached. As the price rises above that point, the option becomes profitable, and the profit increases as the price continues to advance. Once the price reaches the 9.40 level, the taker decides to exercise the call option and thus will be long one contract of July 1983 sugar at 6.20. Simultaneously, one contract of July 1983 sugar will be sold at the market price of 9.40; the net profit on the trade after deducting commissions and the cost of the call is $2,837.

In the above example, sugar hits its peak in January 1983, only one month before the expiration or declaration date. In this case, the taker would normally exercise the option, as opposed to trading against it, because of the short life span remaining. However, if the sugar market had advanced to 9.40 long before February 9, 1983, the taker would have several additional courses of action open to him.

Calls—Trading against Profitable Options

The primary benefit of trading options is the unlimited opportunity for gains with a fixed, relatively moderate risk. Another distinct advantage offered by options is their flexibility or the fact that they can be traded against.

Example A

If the call buyer believes the July 1983 sugar market has advanced as far as it will and that it may decline and not advance again to the 9.40 level before the declaration date, he can lock in his profit by making a short sale of one July 1983 futures contract at 9.40. On the declaration date, the call taker exercises the option, thus establishing a long position at 6.80, and liquidates this long position against the short sale of 9.40, thus realizing the same profit as in the earlier example.

Example B

If the taker feels the market may move lower and then rally again before the declaration date, he will trade against his option by selling short one July 1983 contract at the current level of 9.40. When the market moves lower, the short will be covered by a market purchase. This transaction will generate a profit and leave the original option unchanged. If the market is above the striking price on the declaration date, the call is declared, thus going long at 6.20, and the position is simultaneously liquidated on the market. Thus, the trader has made a profit both on his option and on his trade against the option. If the market is below the original strike price on the declaration date, the option is abandoned and the premium is lost. The premium loss is, of course, offset by the profit made on trading against the option.

Example C

What happens if, after July sugar reaches its peak (9.40 in our example) and the taker has gone short, sugar declines below the call striking price and remains below the striking price on the declaration date? Should this occur, the call would be abandoned and the short covered at the market on the declaration date. The short could, of course, be kept open after the declaration date of the call as a regular future trade, but since we are only concerned here with options and their use, and because holding an unhedged future position creates an additional risk, we will assume that all trading positions are closed on the declaration date.

Example D

What happens to the call option if, on the declaration date, the future is trading at a price higher than the striking price, but below the price at which the premium is fully covered? In this case, it will always benefit the option holder to exercise the option even if the premium is not fully covered. The cash thus generated will reduce the total loss on the option. Suppose, for example, that July sugar is trading at 6.40 on the declaration date:

Sell sugar future at	6.40
Declare call at	− 6.20
Gross transaction profit in points	.20 = 20 points

Transaction profit in points	20
Point value	× 11.20
Transaction profit in dollars	$224.00
Option dealer's commission	− 75.00
Net transaction profit	$149.00

Had the call been abandoned, the loss would have been the total premium cost of $672.00. By declaring the option rather than abandoning it, $149.00 was generated to help reduce the total loss.

Example E

Selling a futures position short against a call not only has the effect of converting the call to a put. In most cases it also maintains the present profit (the difference between the striking price of the call and the price of the short), as long as the short position is held open.

As a rule, while a short is protecting a profit on a call, no further profits can be generated. An exception occurs when the price declines below the striking price of the call. For example, assume a short is entered at 9.40 against a call at 6.20, locking in a profit of 3.20 through all future price levels above the 6.20 striking price of the call. Additional profits are made as soon as the market price declines below the strike price and as long as it remains below that price.

Calls—Trading against Profitable Options

In nearly all of the examples used so far, the call has been profitable at one time during its life. Yet even if an option is never profitable in its own right, profits can be generated by trading against the profitable option.

Suppose an option buyer purchased a call. The anticipated bullish move failed to materialize. A sell signal is given over the near term, so a futures contract is sold short against the call. If the market continues down, the short futures position can be covered profitably and the call can be abandoned on its declaration date since it never reached the strike price.

However, if the market turns up after the future has been sold, the option taker would be subject to a loss equal to the range from where the futures were shorted to the basis, or strike price, of the call. In this example, the maximum additional risk exposure incurred by trading against an unprofitable call, regardless of the height of the rally, would be the difference between the price at which the future was shorted and the strike price of the call.

Purchase Calls—A Stop Order Substitute

Calls can also be used as substitutes for stop-loss orders in the futures. Being uncertain of the duration of the decline and believing a stop could be executed by a short-term technical reaction before the major decline, one might purchase a call in lieu of a stop.

The call provides a permanent stop for all single shorts for six months, meaning that the maximum possible loss, regardless of how high the commodity rises, is the cost of the call. The call also has the advantage in that it places no limit on the potential short side profits.

Calls—Hedges on Profitable Futures

In all of these examples, options were purchased at or before the time at which the futures position was taken as a trade against the option. But the process can be successfully reversed by entering into a futures position and purchasing the option at a later time. The object of this technique is to use an option to protect, or lock in, the present profits of a profitable futures position, while not interfering in any way with the ability of the futures contract to show still further profits.

The speculator with a futures contract can hedge the position and protect the profit with a call. Should the market continue to decline, the speculator can still benefit to the full extent, less the premium cost of the call. The call will be insurance against a loss should the market rise.

Calls—A Hedge on Profitable Puts

This option trading strategy requires an understanding of puts, which are explained in the following discussion.

Put Option Trading Techniques

Purchase Puts—Anticipating Price Decline

A put commodity option is usually purchased because a major decline in the price of the future is anticipated.

Puts—Trading against Profitable Options

Puts allow an investor to profit from a price decline with a fixed and relatively moderate risk. A substantial return can be earned by exercising the profitable put, so the option holder need not attempt even the simplest of trades against the put. Profits can be protected against price rallies by trading long against the put. With this strategy the put remains intact to participate in any further declines once the long position is closed out. For example, assume that a put trader expects a rally but, realizing he could be wrong, watches for signs of continued downward pressure. The price does decline, and the trader profits from the decline by liquidating the long position. By trading against the put instead of exercising it, the taker is able to participate in the additional decline.

Example

What happens if after a market bottoms and the put taker goes long against the put, the market rallies well above the striking price of the put, where it remains until the declaration date? Should this occur, the put would be abandoned and the long sold at the market on the declaration date. It is not necessary to liquidate the long position on the declaration date of the option. But choosing to carry the futures position after the declaration date of the option creates three potential hazards. First, the trader is losing the protection of the option and must, therefore, assume the risk of adverse market movement Second, carrying a naked or unhedged futures position creates the liability of margin calls during periods of adverse market action. And third, if the futures position is held to maturity, there is the problem of taking delivery.

A put should always be declared, even if such declaration will not prove profitable, as long as the exercise generates more dollars than the commission cost to exercise.

Buying a future long against a put has the effect of converting the put to a call. During the period that the long position is kept open, the profit existing on the put at the time a long position is purchased, defined as the difference between the striking price of the put and the price of the long position, is protected. But under most circumstances, no further profits can be made until the long position is liquidated in the market and the put is left unchanged.

Let's summarize some important points. First, note that the buyer of a put will never be called for either original or variation margins on the long positions traded against and protected by the put option. Remember also that purchasing a futures contract against a put converts the put into a call. While the long position is maintained, profit is defined as the difference between the strike price of the put and the price at which the long futures contract was purchased. This profit is totally protected, and there is a very real possibility that the futures price will rise above the strike price of the put, thus generating additional profits. Finally, keep in mind that by trading against a put one avoids having to exercise it when the put is profitable but a temporary price rally is imminent.

Purchase Puts—A Stop Order Substitute

An option has many advantages over a stop. Like a stop, an option provides protection at a guaranteed price, but there is no limit to the number of times an option can be used as a stop. An option can be reversed, meaning that a put can become a call and vice versa. An option also provides protection against whipsaws.

Puts—Hedges on Profitable Futures

A put used as a hedge against a profitable futures position protects profit by allowing the long position to be offset against the short created by declaration of the put at the put striking price. The protection offered by the put is not affected by whipsaws, the number of declines, or their severity. The protection lasts through the life of the put, so only the ultimate move is important. The put also permits the futures holder to profit from additional strength while having the peace of mind that, regardless of future market action, his current profit is locked into a protected position.

Puts—Hedges on Calls

If the market does drop, the put is exercised in order to protect the call's profit. More importantly, the put does not interfere with the future's ability to profit further from a continuation of the bull movement. The cost of this protection, without jeopardizing future profits, is still only the premium cost. Compare this to a futures hedge, using a short in another contract month that moves in a one-to-one linear relationship. When using futures to hedge futures, the premium cost of the option is saved, but no additional profits are possible, regardless of how high or low the future ultimately trades.

The second side of the option hedging option concept is the use of a call to hedge a profitable put position. Should the market rise, the call can be profitably exercised. If the bearish move continues unabated, additional profits can be generated. The cost of this hedge is simply the premium cost of the call.

The Special Double

The special double option is simply a combination of a put option and a call option which allows the purchaser to either buy or sell (but not both) a commodity at a fixed strike price for future delivery at any time prior to the declaration date. While only one side of the double can ultimately be exercised or declared, both sides can be traded against as desired. Every trading strategy discussed with regard to puts and calls, including the use of an option to hedge another option, options as hedges on futures, trading against unprofitable options, and the use of options in lieu of stop orders, will work equally well with either or both sides of the double.

The Unique Advantages of Double Options

The double option is one of the most exciting investment vehicles to emerge in recent years. The double option offers all the advantages of puts and calls, including their minimum and calculable risk exposure, tremendous leverage, unlimited profit potential, and freedom from margin calls. But the double has an additional advantage. The purchaser of a put must attempt to predict the market. Except where the put is used in lieu of a stop to protect a new long position, or to hedge a profitable long position, the put buyer is anticipating a substantial drop in price. Likewise, the speculator who purchases a naked call, not intending to use it immediately as a stop for a short futures position or as a hedge for a profitable short, is anticipating a major price move on the upside. The unique advantage of the double is that it frees the holder from dependence on market direction. The double option, combining both a put and a call, can be profitable regardless of whether the market advances or declines. It is far easier to determine volatility than price direction.

C

GLOSSARY
OF TERMS

ACTUALS: The physical or cash commodity, as distinguished from commodity futures contracts.

ARBITRAGE: The simultaneous purchase of one commodity against the sale of another in order to profit from distortions from usual price relationships. (See also spread, straddle.)

BASIS: The difference between the cash or spot price and the price of the nearby futures contract.

BID: An offer to buy a specific quantity of a commodity at a stated price.

BROAD TAPE: Term commonly applied to newswires carrying price and background information on securities and commodities markets, in contrast to the exchanges' own price transmission wires, which use a narrow ticker tape.

BROKER: A person paid a fee or commission for acting as an agent in making contracts or sales; floor broker—in commodities futures trading, a person who actually executes orders on the trading floor of an exchange; account executive (associated person)—the person who deals with customers and their orders in commission house offices. (See registered commodity representative.)

BROKERAGE: A fee charged by a broker for execution of a transaction, an amount per transaction or a percentage of the total value of the transaction; usually referred to as a commission fee.

BUCKET, BUCKETING: Illegal practice of accepting orders to buy or sell without executing such orders; and the illegal use of the customer's margin deposit without disclosing the fact of such use.

BUY OR SELL ON CLOSE OR OPENING: To buy or sell at the end or the beginning of the trading session at a price without disclosing the fact of such use.

BUYING HEDGE (or LONG HEDGE): Buying futures contracts to protect against possible increased cost of commodities which will be needed in the future (See hedging.)

CARRYING CHARGES: Costs incurred in warehousing the physical commodity, generally including interest, insurance, and storage.

CARRYOVER: That part of the current supply of a commodity consisting of stocks from previous production/marketing seasons.

CASH COMMODITY: Actual stocks of a commodity, as distinguished from futures contracts; goods available for immediate delivery or delivery within a specified period following sale; or a commodity bought or sold with an agreement for delivery at a specified future date. (See actuals and forward contracting.)

CASH FORWARD SALE: See forward contracting

CERTIFICATED STOCK: Stocks of a commodity that have been inspected and found to be of a quality deliverable against futures contracts, stored at the delivery points designated as regular or acceptable for delivery by the commodity exchange.

CHARTING: The use of graphs and charts in the technical analysis of futures markets to plot trends of price movements, average movements of price, volume, and open interest. (See technical analysis.)

CLEARINGHOUSE: An agency connected with commodity exchanges through which all futures contracts are made, offset, or fulfilled through delivery of the actual commodity and through which financial settlement is made; often is a fully chartered separate corporation, rather than a division of the exchange proper.

CLEARING PRICE: See settlement price.

CLOSING RANGE: A range of closely related prices at which transactions took place at the closing of the market; buy and sell orders at the closing might have been filled at any point within such a range.

COMMISSION MERCHANT: One who makes a trade, either for another member of the exchange or for a nonmember client, but who makes the trade in his or her own name and becomes liable as principal to the other party to the transaction.

COMMODITY FUTURES TRADING COMMISSION (CFTC): A regulatory commission set up by Congress to administer the Commodity Exchange Act, which supervises trading on commodity exchanges that are regulated as contract markets.

CONTRACT GRADES: Standards or grades of commodities listed in the rules of the exchanges which must be met when delivering cash commodities against futures contracts. Grades are often accompanied by a schedule of discounts and premiums allowable for delivery of commodities of lesser or greater quality than the contract grade.

CORNER: To secure such relative control of a commodity that its price can be manipulated.

COVER: To offset a previous futures transaction with an equal and opposite transaction. Short covering is a purchase of futures contracts to cover an earlier sale of an equal number of the same delivery month; liquidation is the sale of futures contracts to offset the obligation to take delivery on an equal number of futures contracts of the same delivery month purchased earlier.

CURRENT DELIVERY (MONTH): The futures contract which will come to maturity and become deliverable during the current month; also called "spot month."

DAY TRADERS: Commodity traders, generally members of the exchange active on the trading floor, who take positions in commodities and then liquidate them prior to the close of the trading day.

DEFAULT: In reference to the federal farm loan program, the decision on the part of a producer of commodities not to repay the government loan, but instead to surrender his or her crops; in futures markets, the theoretical failure of a party to a futures contract to either make or take delivery of the physical commodity as required under the contract.

DELIVERABLE GRADES: See contract grades.

DELIVERY MONTH: A calendar month during which a futures contract matures and becomes deliverable.

DELIVERY NOTICE: Notice from the clearinghouse of a seller's intention to deliver the physical commodity against a short futures position; precedes and is distinct from the warehouse receipt or shipping certificate, which is the instrument of transfer of ownership.

DELIVERY POINTS: Those locations designated by commodity exchanges at which stocks of a commodity represented by a futures contract may be delivered in fulfillment of the contract.

DELIVERY PRICE: The official settlement price of the trading session during which the buyer of futures contracts receives through the clearinghouse a notice of the seller's intention to deliver, and the price at which the buyer must pay for the commodities represented by the futures contract.

DISCOUNT: A downward adjustment in price allowed for delivery of stocks of a commodity of lesser than deliverable grade against a futures contract; sometimes used to refer to the price difference between futures of different delivery months, as in the phrase "July at a discount to May," indicating that the price of the July future is lower than that of the May.

DISCRETIONARY ACCOUNT: An arrangement by which the holder of the account gives written power of attorney to another, often a broker, to make buying and selling decisions without notification to the holder; often referred to as a managed account or controlled account.

ELASTICITY: A characteristic of commodities which describes the interaction of the supply, demand, and price of a commodity. A commodity is said to be elastic in demand when a price change creates an increase or decrease in consumption. The supply of a commodity is said to be elastic when a change in price creates change in the production of the commodity. Inelasticity of supply or demand exists when either supply or demand is relatively unresponsive to changes in price.

F.O.B.: Free on board; indicates that all delivery, inspection, and elevation or loading costs involved in putting commodities on board a carrier have been paid.

FEED RATIOS: The variable relationships of the cost of feeding animals to market weight sales prices, expressed in ratios, such as the hog/corn ratio. These serve as indicators of the profit return or lack of it in feeding animals to market weight.

FIRST NOTICE DAY: First day on which notices of intention to deliver cash commodities against futures contracts can be presented by sellers and received by buyers through the exchange clearinghouse.

FORWARDING CONTRACTING: A cash transaction common in many industries, including commodity merchandising, in which the buyer and seller agree upon delivery of a specified quality and quantity of goods at a specified future date. A specific price may be agreed upon in advance or there may be agreement that the price will be determined at the time of delivery on the basis of either the prevailing local cash price or a futures price.

FREE SUPPLY: Stocks of a commodity which are available for commercial sale, as distinguished from government-owned or controlled stocks.

FUNDAMENTAL ANALYSIS: An approach to analysis of futures markets and commodity futures price trends which examines the underlying factors which will affect the supply and demand of the commodity being traded in futures contract. (See also technical analysis.)

GROSS PROCESSING MARGIN (GPM): Refers to the difference between the cost of soybeans and the combined sales income of the soybean oil and meal which results from processing soybeans.

HEDGING: The sale of futures contracts in anticipation of future sales of cash commodities as a protection against possible price declines, or the purchase of futures contracts in anticipation of future purchases of cash commodities as a protection against increasing costs. (See also buying hedge, selling hedge.)

INVERTED MARKET: Futures market in which the nearer months are selling at premiums over the more distant months; characteristically, a market in which supplies are currently in shortage.

INVISIBLE SUPPLY: Uncounted stocks of a commodity in the hands of wholesalers, manufacturers, and producers which cannot be identified accurately; stocks outside commercial channels but theoretically available to the market.

LAST TRADING DAY: Day on which trading ceases for the maturing (current) delivery month.

LIFE OF CONTRACT: Period between the beginning of trading in a particular future and the expiration of trading in the delivery month.

LIMIT ORDER: An order in which the customer sets a limit on either price or time of execution, or both, as contrasted with a market order, which implies that the order should be filled at the most favorable price as soon as possible.

LIQUID MARKET: A market where selling and buying can be accomplished easily due to the presence of many interested buyers and sellers.

LOAN PROGRAM: Primary means of government agricultural price support operations, in which the government lends money to farmers at announced rates, with crops used as collateral. Default on these loans is the primary method by which the government acquires stocks of agricultural commodities.

LONG: One who has bought a cash commodity or a commodity futures contract, in contrast to a short, who has sold a cash commodity or futures contract.

MARGIN: 1. An amount of money deposited by both buyers and sellers of futures contracts to ensure performance against the contract, i.e., to deliver to take delivery of the commodity (not an equity or down payment for the goods represented by the futures contract). 2. Profit margin—the difference between the price one pays for goods and the price at which the goods or their byproducts are resold.

MARGIN CALL: A call from a brokerage firm to a customer to bring margin deposits back up to minimum levels required by exchange regulations; similarly, a request by the clearinghouse to a clearing member firm to make additional deposits to bring clearing margins back to minimum levels required by clearinghouse rules.

MARKET ORDER: An order to buy or sell futures contracts which is to be filled at the best possible price and as soon as possible. In contrast to a limit order, which may specify requirements for price or time of execution. (See also limit order.)

MATURITY: Period within which a futures contract can be settled by delivery of the actual commodity; the period between the first notice day and the last trading day of a commodity futures contract.

NEARBY DELIVERY (MONTH): The futures contract closest to maturity.

NOMINAL PRICE: Declared price for a futures month sometimes used in place of a closing price when no recent trading has taken place in that particular delivery month; usually an average of the bid and asked prices.

NOTICE DAY: See first notice day.

NOTICE OF DELIVERY: See delivery notice.

OFFER: An indication of willingness to sell at a given price; opposite of bid.

OFFSET: The liquidation of a purchase of futures through the sale of an equal number of contracts of the same delivery months, or the covering of a short sale of futures contract through the purchase of an equal number of contracts of the same delivery month. Either action transfers the obligation to make or take delivery of the actual commodity to other persons.

OMNIBUS ACCOUNT: An account carried by one futures commission merchant with another in which the transactions of two or more persons are combined rather than designated separately and the identity of the individual accounts is not disclosed.

OPEN INTEREST: The total number of futures contracts of a given commodity which have not yet been offset by opposite futures transactions nor fulfilled by delivery of the actual commodity; the total number of open transactions, with each transaction having a buyer and a seller.

OPEN OUTCRY: Method of public auction for making bids and offers in the trading pits or rings of commodity exchanges.

OPENING RANGE: Range of closely related prices at which transactions took place at the opening of the market; buying and selling orders at the opening might be filled at any point within such a range.

ORIGINAL MARGIN: Term applied to the initial deposit of margin money required of clearing member firms by clearinghouse rules; parallel to the initial margin deposit required of customers by exchange regulations.

OVERBOUGHT: A technical opinion that the market price has risen too steeply and too fast in relation to underlying fundamental factors.

OVERSOLD: A technical opinion that the market price has declined too steeply and too fast in relation to underlying fundamental factors.

P & S (purchase and sale) STATEMENT: A statement sent by a commission house to a customer when his or her futures position has changed, showing the number of contracts involves, the prices at which the contracts were bought or sold, the gross profit or loss, the commission charges, and the net profit or loss on the transactions.

PARITY: A theoretically equal relationship between farm product prices and all other prices. In farm program legislation, parity is defined in such a manner that the purchasing power of a unit of an agricultural commodity is maintained at its level during and earlier historical base period.

POSITION: A market commitment. A buyer of futures contracts is said to have a long position and, conversely, a seller of futures contracts is said to have a short position.

POSITION LIMIT: The maximum number of futures contracts in certain regulated commodities that one can hold, according to the provisions of the CFTC.

POSITION TRADER: A commodity trader who either buys or sells contracts and holds them for an extended period of time, as distinguished from the day trader, who will normally initiate and liquidate a futures position within a single trading session.

PREMIUM: The additional payment allowed by exchange regulations for delivery or higher-than-required standards or grades of a commodity against a futures contract. In speaking of price relationships between different delivery months of a given commodity, one is said to be trading at a premium over another when its price is greater than that of the other.

PRICE LIMIT: Maximum price advance or decline from the previous day settlement price permitted for a commodity in one trading session by the rules of the exchange.

PRIVATE WIRES: Wires leased by various firms and news agencies for the transmission of information to branch offices and subscriber clients.

PRODUCER: Farmer who grows crops, etc.

PUBLIC ELEVATORS: Grain storage facilities, licensed and regulated by state and federal agencies, in which space is rented out to whomever is willing to pay for it; some are also approved by the commodity exchanges as regular for delivery of commodities against futures contracts.

PYRAMIDING: The use of profits on existing futures positions as margins to increase the size of the position, normally in successively smaller increments; such as the use of profits on the purchase of five futures contracts as margin to purchase an additional four contracts, whose profits will in turn be used to margin an additional three contracts.

RANGE: The difference between the highest and lowest prices recorded during a given trading session, week, month, year, etc.

REPORTING LIMIT: Sizes of positions set by the exchanges and/or by the CFTC at or above which commodity traders must make daily reports to the exchange and/or the CFTC as to the size of the position by commodity, by delivery month, and according to the purpose of trading, i.e., speculative or hedging.

RETENDER: The right of holders of futures contract who have been tendered a delivery notice through the clearinghouse to offer the notice for sale on the open market, liquidating their obligation to take delivery under the contract; applicable only to certain commodities and only within a specified period of time.

ROUND LOT: A quantity of a commodity equal in size to the corresponding futures contract for the commodity, as distinguished from a job lot, which may be larger or smaller than the contract.

ROUND TURN: The combination of an initiating purchase or sale of a futures contract and offsetting sale or purchase of an equal number of futures contracts ot the same delivery month. Commission fees for commodity transactions cover the round turn.

SAMPLE GRADE: In commodities, usually the lowest quality acceptable for delivery in satisfaction of futures contracts. (See contract grades.)

SCALPER: A speculator on the trading floor of an exchange who buys and sells rapidly, with small profits or losses, holding positions for only a short time during a trading session. Typically, a scalper will stand ready to buy at a fraction below the last transaction price and to sell at a fraction above, thus creating market liquidity.

SELLING HEDGE (OR SHORT HEDGE): Selling futures contracts to protect against possible decreased prices of commodities which will be sold in the future.(See hedging).

SETTLEMENT PRICE: The closing price, or a price within the range of closing prices, which is used as the official price in determining net gains or losses at the close of each trading session.

SHORT: One who has sold a cash commodity or a commodity futures contract, in contrast to a long, who has bought a cash commodity or futures contract.

SPECULATOR: One who attempts to anticipate commodity price changes and make profits through the sale and/or purchase of commodity futures contracts. A speculator with a forecast of advancing prices hopes to profit by buying futures contracts and then liquidating the obligation to take delivery with a later sale of an equal number of futures of the same delivery month at a higher price. A speculator with a forecast of declining prices hopes to profit by selling commodity futures contracts and then covering the obligation to deliver with a later purchase of futures at a lower price.

SPOT COMMODITY: See cash commodity.

SPREAD (or STRADDLE): The purchase of one futures delivery month against the sale of another futures delivery month of the same commodity; the purchase of one delivery month of one commodity against the sale of that same delivery month of a different commodity; or the purchase of one commodity in one market against the sale of that commodity in another market, to take advantage of and profit from the distortions from the normal price relationships that sometimes occur. The term is also used to refer to the difference between the price of one futures month and the price of another month of the same commodity. (See also arbitrage.)

SWITCH: Liquidation of a position in one delivery month of a commodity and simultaneous initiation of a similar position in another delivery month of the same commodity. When used by hedgers, this tactic is referred to as "rolling forward" the hedge.

TECHNICAL ANALYSIS: An approach to analysis of futures markets and likely future trends of commodity prices which examines the technical factors of market activity. Technicians normally examine patterns of price change, rates of change, and changes in volume of trading and open interest. This data is often charted to show trends and formations which will in turn serve as indicators of likely future price movements.

TENDER: The act on the part of the seller of futures contracts of giving notice to the clearinghouse that he or she intends to deliver the physical commodity in satisfaction of the futures contract. The clearinghouse in turn passes along the notice to oldest buyer of record in that delivery month of the commodity (See also retender.)

TICKER TAPE: A continuous paper tape transmission of commodity or security prices, volume and other trading and market information which operates on private or leased wires by the exchanges, available to their member firms and other interested parties on a subscription basis.

TO-ARRIVE CONTRACT: A type of deferred shipment in which the price is based on delivery at the destination point and the seller pays the freight in shipping it to that point.

TRANSFERABLE NOTICE: See retender.

VARIATION MARGIN CALL: A mid-season call by the clearinghouse on a clearing member requiring the deposit of additional funds to bring clearing margin monies up to minimum levels in relation to changing prices and the clearing member's net position.

WAREHOUSE RECEIPT: Document guaranteeing the existence and availability of a given quantity and quality of a commodity in storage; commonly used as the instrument of transfer of ownership in both cash and futures transactions.

PRACTICE EXAMINATIONS

Trading Attitude Survey

The following questions have no right or wrong answers, but they indicate the emotional qualities you'll need to be a successful commodity futures trader.

1. Suppose you are going to a movie for which you can't get advance tickets. You find a long line of people waiting outside the theater, but you are very interested in seeing the movie. What is your action?
   a. Wait in line.
   b. Try to get ahead of the others in line.
   c. Leave and do something else.
   d. Try to pay someone to allow you to take his or her position in line.

2. You have decided to buy a new car and have examined the pros and cons of various models. Tomorrow you'll pick up the model that you have selected, but this evening you are with friends. When you mention your decision, they start citing examples that suggest your choice is ill advised. What is your action?
   a. You argue vehemently in favor of your choice.
   b. You abandon your previous selection and resign yourself to looking for a more suitable car.
   c. You listen courteously to your friends, offer little argument, and the next day pick up the car as you had planned.
   d. You decide to renegotiate the terms of the purchase of the car on the basis of the new information your friends gave you.

3. Select the three words that best describe how you view yourself and your actions.

   a. Aggressive   d. Impulsive
   b. Reserved   e. Uncompromising
   c. Patient   f. Tolerant

4. Select the three words that best describe how you think other people view you and your actions.

   a. Aggressive   d. Impulsive
   b. Reserved   e. Uncompromising
   c. Patient   f. Tolerant

5. What do you define as risk capital?
   a. All liquid assets.
   b. All the money in your investment account.
   c. The amount of money that would not cause a severe hardship to lose.
   d. The amount of money that if lost would have no impact on your financial well-being.

Practice Exam A

1. The effect of speculation is to:
   A. Increase price fluctuations
   B. Alter supply to demand forces
   C. Reduce farmer risk in growing his crop
   D. Reduce range of cash price fluctuation

2. The major distinction between cash and futures contracts is:
   A. Offset procedure
   B. To-arrive provisions
   C. Inspection procedures
   D. Commodity grade

3. The concept of futures trading was used in Europe long before U.S. markets were developed:
   A. True
   B. False

4. A cash forward sale is essentially the same as a futures contract with the major difference being the ability to offset in futures:
   A. True
   B. False

5. Cash forward and futures contracts differ in that:
   A. The latter are traded on organized exchanges, but the former need not be
   B. Futures contracts are standardized and cash forward contracts are frequently negotiated
   C. Futures can be more easily offset
   D. All of the above.

6. The motive of the speculator is profit:
   A. True
   B. False

7. The efficiency of a market is most influenced by:
   A. The number of traders
   B. The weather

C. The availability of cash supplies

D. The amount of margin requirements

8. On the purchase or sale of a futures contract, transfer of ownership is not accomplished unless:

A. 50 percent of the cash value of the contract has been deposited

B. The commodity position is offset

C. The commodity is actually delivered

D. It is done via a regulated commodity exchange

9. The cash market and the nearest futures contract tend to converge:

A. At the country elevator

B. At the end of the month

C. At terminal markets

D. During the delivery month

10. If a futures contract is offset, delivery is required immediately:

A. True

B. False

11. If a farmer wants to hedge his crop, he would buy futures:

A. True

B. False

12. The most important function of a futures market is:

A. Forward pricing

B. Attracting speculators

C. Assembling, standardizing, and grading

D. Eliminating all risk

13. About 98 percent of all futures contracts are satisfied by offset and not delivery:

A. True

B. False

14. The efficiency of a market is determined by:

A. The number of open contracts

B. The number of traders

C. The contract details

D. All of the above.

15. Without a futures market in which to hedge, the price of a loaf of bread probably would be:

A. Higher

B. Lower

C. Makes no difference

D. Always stabilized

16. In selling futures against a growing crop, one is said to be assuming the role of a:
    A. Speculator
    B. Hedger
    C. Spreader
    D. Gambler

17. Anybody who is engaged in a business that is subject to price fluctuation is a:
    A. Hedger
    B. Scalper
    C. Processor
    D. Speculator

18. A hedge position:
    A. Eliminates chance of profit
    B. Increases need for working capital
    C. Shifts risk to another
    D. All of the above

19. To hedge against a forward cash sale you would:
    A. Sell futures
    B. Make a substitute sale
    C. Buy futures
    D. Arbitrage

20. An individual who does not own or have access to storage facilities should not trade in futures:
    A. True
    B. False

21. A short hedge protects against:
    A. Rising prices
    B. Falling prices
    C. Both technically
    D. None of the above

22. When buying or selling a futures contract, one is contingently liable for:
    A. Original margin
    B. 70 percent of total contract value
    C. Total contract value
    D. None of the above

23. A cash forward contract differs from a futures contract primarily in that:
    A. A cash forward contract is usually more personal
    B. A futures contract can be more easily offset
    C. The cash contract is the result of arbitration
    D. A futures contract is almost always the result of open outcry

24. The function of the speculator is to provide liquidity:
    A. True
    B. False

25. A commodity futures short sale may be made:
    A. By anyone at anytime
    B. Uptick
    C. No tick
    D. Downtick

Practice Exam B

1. A cash sale can involve a forward contract:
   A. True
   B. False

2. Which of the following is not considered a part of carrying charges:
   A. Storage costs
   B. Interest
   C. Transportation
   D. Insurance

3. Hedging may be defined as "a futures buy or sell in the expectation of making a merchandising transaction in the future":
   A. True
   B. False

4. When a futures contract is offset, delivery is made immediately:
   A. True
   B. False

5. When a futures price is more than the cash price, the market is called:
   A. Inverted
   B. Reverse
   C. Discount
   D. Premium

6. A person who holds an inventory would hedge by:
   A. Making a substitute purchase
   B. Making cash forward purchase
   C. Entering into a to-arrive contract
   D. Selling futures (a substitute sale)

7. An individual who buys futures against cash forward sales is a:
   A. Spreader
   B. Scalper
   C. Hedger
   D. Trader

8. The term "ex-pit" is essentially the same as "against actuals" (AA) and "exchange for physicals" (EFP):
   A. True
   B. False

9. The hedger will usually pay a smaller margin than speculative longs and shorts:
   A. True
   B. False

10. A selling hedge at a full carrying charge premium is almost always worthwhile because:
    A. It gives price protection regardless of whether prices subsequently rise or fall
    B. When prices are rising, the value of spot usually rise more than futures
    C. When prices are falling, the value of spot usually declines less than futures
    D. An adverse basis change is unimportant

11. Cash and futures prices will tend to converge during the delivery month:
    A. True
    B. False

12. Trade margins are usually lower than those for speculative customers because:
    A. They are subject to smaller price fluctuations
    B. They are financially more stable
    C. There is less risk in their position
    D. The statement is not true

13. A grain dealer who makes a forward cash sale would hedge by:
    A. Selling cash
    B. Buying futures
    C. Selling futures
    D. Making a bid

14. Cash transactions always involve forward contracts:
    A. True
    B. False

15. A grain elevator operator who hedges generally intends to deliver against a futures contract he sells:
    A. True
    B. False

16. A hedger who is long a contract of December wheat has in effect made a(n):
    A. Substitute sale
    B. Inverted hedge
    C. Substitute purchase
    D. Speculation

17. A futures hedge involves having a short futures position when one owns the cash commodity and a long futures position when the cash commodity is needed:
    A. True
    B. False

18. With a buying hedge in futures:
    A. Interest costs on money used to finance inventory tend to be greater
    B. Working capital needs are smaller
    C. The hedger usually will accept delivery of the commodities tendered so as to minimize his costs
    D. Basis changes are not important

19. A buy hedge would be used by:
    A. A farmer to protect his crop
    B. A grain elevator operator to protect his inventory
    C. An exporter to protect his sales
    D. None of the above.

20. Hedging techniques only work effectively for the short term:
    A. True
    B. False

21. A hedge position may not give full protection against adverse price movements because:
    A. During the time the hedge is operative the basis may change
    B. Cash prices and futures prices usually move in unison
    C. The various futures months do not usually sell at the same price
    D. Transportation costs vary from one area to the next

22. A long hedge is actually a(n):
    A. Substitute sale
    B. Insurance procedure
    C. Substitute purchase
    D. Speculation

23. If a seller delivers against his short future position with better than contract grade, the buyer may be required to pay a designated premium for it:
    A. True
    B. False

24. Unless offset, a contract calls for delivery of a specific quantity and grade(s) of a commodity:
    A. True
    B. False

25. A delivery notice issued by a short constitutes a change in ownership of the cash commodity:
    A. True
    B. False

26. The buyer has the right to demand delivery at anytime during the delivery period:
    A. True
    B. False

Practice Exam C

1. An order to buy 5 May wheat on the Chicago Board of Trade placed with one broker and a simultaneous order to sell 5 May wheat on the Chicago Board of Trade placed with another broker is:
    A. An intramarket spread
    B. An intermarket spread
    C. An intercommodity spread
    D. A wash sale

2. A grain elevator operator receives delivery of 3 million bushels of wheat on May 1, for which he pays $2.00 a bushel. At the same time, he enters into a commitment to buy an additional 1 million bushels for delivery on June 1 at $2.10 a bushel. The elevator operator would most likely:
    A. Hedge 3 million bushels on May 1 and 1,000,000 bushels on June 1 by buying futures
    B. Hedge 3 million bushels on May 1 and 1,000,000 bushels on June 1 by selling futures
    C. Hedge 4 million bushels on May 1 by buying futures
    D. Hedge 4 million bushels on May 1 by selling futures

3.

Date	Cash	Futures Price (July)	Basis
10/3	$126\frac{1}{2}$	$145\frac{3}{4}$	$-19\frac{1}{4}$
1/3	$131\frac{1}{2}$	$145\frac{3}{4}$	$-14\frac{1}{4}$

What is the net basis gain for a sell hedger during the period October 3 and January 3:
    A. -5
    B. Nothing
    C. $+\frac{3}{4}$
    D. $+5$¢

Use the following information to answer Questions 4 and 5:

The price of cash on August 1 is $2.20.
The price of September futures is $2.30.
The price of December futures is $2.40.

4. If a hedger who is long on the basis were to sell September futures, his basis would be:
   A. 10 cents over
   B. 10 cents under
   C. 20 cents over
   D. 20 cents under

5. If a hedger who is short on the basis were to buy December futures, his basis would be:
   A. 10 cents over
   B. 10 cents under
   C. 20 cents over
   D. 20 cents under

Use the following table for questions 6, 7, and 8.

Date	Cash	Futures	Basis
Oct 1	$149\frac{1}{2}$	$159\frac{1}{2}$	− 10
Nov 3	$149\frac{1}{4}$	$162\frac{1}{2}$	− $13\frac{1}{4}$
Dec 1	151	160	− 9
Dec 24	160	184	− 24

6. If someone who needed a cash commodity bought futures as a hedge on December 1 and liquidated the hedge on December 24, the hedge would have contributed how much profit to his operation:
   A. Plus 15
   B. Plus 24
   C. Plus 9
   D. No profit; in fact, a loss

7. If the sell hedge was established on November 3 and liquidated on December 1, the results would have been:
   A. Plus $2\frac{1}{2}$
   B. Plus $4\frac{1}{4}$
   C. Plus $1\frac{3}{4}$
   D. Plus $3\frac{1}{4}$

8. If the cash commodity was owned and if futures were sold as a hedge on October 1 and liquidated on November 3, how much would the hedge have contributed or cost with relation to his carrying charges:
   A. Minus $3\frac{1}{4}$

B. Plus $3\frac{1}{4}$
C. Minus $13\frac{1}{4}$
D. Minus 3

Use the following information to answer questions 9, 10, and 11.

Date	Cash Wheat	Jan. Wheat Futures	Basis
July	1.35	1.50	– 15
Sept	1.40	1.40	0
Dec	1.42	1.47	– 5
Jan	1.43	1.40	+ 3

9. For a wheat elevator, how much would a hedge placed in July and lifted in September contribute towards carrying charges?
    A. – 5¢
    B. – 15¢
    C. 5¢
    D. 15¢

10. How much if placed in September and lifted in December?
    A. – 5¢
    B. – 15¢
    C. 15¢

11. How much if placed in September and kept to expiration?
    A. – 5¢
    B. 0
    C. 3¢
    D. 13¢

12. A plywood dealer enters an order with a mill to purchase plywood for delivery in three months, with the price of the plywood to be based on the price on the day of delivery. The plywood dealer hedges by buying futures. The price of futures is $104 and the price of cash is $110. On the day the cash plywood is delivered, the price of the cash plywood is $116 and the price of the futures is $120. The hedge resulted in a:
    A. $6 profit
    B. $6 loss
    C. $10 profit
    D. $10 loss

Practice Exam D

1. A spreader who is bullish on a commodity would consider:
    A. Selling the near and buying a deferred month
    B. Buying the near and selling a deferred month

    C. Could never calculate his spread risk

    D. None of the above

2. Spot, cash, physicals, and actuals all refer to essentially the same thing:
   A. True
   B. False

3. In a normal market where the difference between more distant and near futures is expected to narrow a spreader would:
   A. Buy near future, sell distant future
   B. Tighten supply picture.
   C. Take no action
   D. Sell short

4. A spreader who has purchased December wheat and sold March wheat on the same exchange has established:
   A. An inter-market spread
   B. An inter-commodity spread
   C. An inter-delivery spread
   D. A commodity-product

5. The inter-delivery (or intra-market) spread is the most popular spread:
   A. True
   B. False

6. If the near month is at a premium over the far month and you expect the spread tomorrow, you would as a spreader:
   A. Buy the near and sell the far
   B. Enter into a limited risk spread
   C. Sell the near and buy the far
   D. Sell the far and buy the near

7. In a spread position:
   A. There is always a predictable risk
   B. There is only a limited profit opportunity
   C. There is no limit to the risk involved when you sell a near and buy a far month
   D. Carrying charges always prevail between a near month and a far month

8. Speculators normally avoid a thin market:
   A. True
   B. False

9. An intramarket spread requires there be no more than one market:
   A. True
   B. False

10. In a normal market, if a spreader expects a narrowing of the spread he would:
    A. Do nothing
    B. Buy the near and sell the deferred

    C. Sell the near and buy the far

    D. B or C

11. A spreader who sold March corn and bought May corn when futures were inverted, would have:

    A. Unlimited profit potential

    B. Unlimited risk

    C. No profit potential

    D. No risk

12. Spread positions usually require less margin because:

    A. Price changes between futures months are less than flat price risks

    B. The two months involved always move up and down together

    C. There is virtually no risk

    D. All except A

13. Pyramiding is the practice of using accrued paper profits as margin for additional trading positions:

    A. True

    B. False

14. The purchase of May wheat in Chicago and sale of May wheat in Kansas City is an:

    A. Intermarket spread

    B. Interdelivery spread

    C. Intramarket spread

    D. None of the above

15. An individual who simultaneously buys soybeans and sells oil and meal has effected a reverse crush spread:

    A. True

    B. False

16. A reverse crush hedge involves buying soybean oil and selling soybeans and meal futures:

    A. True

    B. False

17. A soybean processor who buys soybeans and sells the products in the futures market would be placing a(n):

    A. Reverse crush

    B. Processor conversion

    C. Crush hedge (putting on crush)

    D. Intracommodity spread

18. A speculator who sells soybeans and buys SBM and SBO would initiate what is known as a:

    A. Hedge

    B. Spread

C. Crushing spread
D. Reverse crush (BOM) spread

19. If December wheat is selling at a premium to March wheat of the following year and a spreader believes the spread will narrow, he would:
A. Sell December and buy March
B. Sell March and buy December
C. Forget it
D. None of the above

20. A soybean processor who buys beans and oil and sells meal has a crush spread:
A. True
B. False

21. A customer simultaneously transferring a short from one contract month to another month in the same commodity executes a:
A. Switch
B. Straddle
C. Net trade
D. None of the above

22. A person who is long and short a commodity is a:
A. Spreader
B. Speculator
C. Hedger
D. None of the above

23. A spread can be:
A. Between different markets, same commodities
B. Within same market, different commodities
C. Between same commodities, different months
D. All of the above

ANSWER KEY

Trading Attitude Survey

To see how your modus operandi will help or hinder you as a commodity trader, check your answers against the analysis below. If answer was:

1.a. You are obviously patient and willing to wait for what you want, but you run the risk of being drawn into the popular solution. Following the crowd can be a dangerous activity. Your challenge is to know when to hold your ground.

1.b. Although this may seem to be a discourteous act, in commodity trading your purpose is to be ahead of the crowd. You may find yourself in the wrong crowd from time to time or you may be denied entry. Your biggest risk may be discovering when to leave.

1.c. Your impatience is healthy if you use it to avoid following the crowd, but it can be a problem if you are impulsive as a defense against having to wait.

1.d. As a commodity trader, you'll have to become accustomed to paying for what you get. You seem to be willing to do that, but don't try to buy success. The markets have far more money than you do.

2.a. Sticking to your guns is commendable as long as you are supporting your convictions with logic and are not rationalizing. Talking your position can have one of two purposes: convincing others that you are right or convincing you that you are right.

2.b. Admitting that you are wrong is an important action as a trader. The risk is letting others convince you that you are wrong and abandoning your convictions.
Perhaps you should adjust your "usual fashion" of examining the pros and cons to give you stronger convictions.

2.c. This is the most common characteristic of successful traders. The difficulty as a beginning trader is to know what to filter out and what to acknowledge.

2.d. Using information to adjust your trade is not without merit but may give you the signal that your original examiniation techniques are flawed.

3.a.d.e. This combination suggests that you are what the business psychologist calls a "Type A" individual. Type As are great leaders and often end up in positions of power. They do not make particularly good traders until they learn to control their aggressiveness. Type As are generally great at delegating if they allow themselves the luxury and would probably do well to select someone else to manage their commodity account. As a trader, you'll be best in short-term positions.

3.b.c.f. This combination can be dangerous if accompanied by a lack of commitment. These are the characteristics of a listener, but if the learned information is not used to implement action then nothing is gained. As a trader, you'll be best in long-term positions.

3.a. Aggressive: You run the risk of trying to "muscle" the market. "I'll keep buying until the market goes up." You will run out of money before the market runs out of prices.

3.b. Reserved: If you are reserved, as in calculating, this is positive to your trading. If you are reserved, as in timid, the commodity markets may not be the place for you.

3.c. Patient: There is a fine line between patient and apathetic. Waiting for the right conditions for a trade is virtuous, but don't let the lack of positive action be expressed as apathy.

3.d. Impulsive: This characteristic may be the most dangerous of all. The emotion that inspires impulsiveness is the one that allows you to take positions that are not very well thought out. When you feel the most right is probably when you are wrong.

3.e. Uncompromising: this can be a very valuable trait in selecting a trading technique or trading advisor, but it can be your doom if you can't admit you are wrong.

3.f. Tolerant: While you are learning, this trait will help you adjust your thinking. A pliable mind absorbs more rapidly. As you trade, redirect your tolerance to avoid letting the intraday market "noise" disturb your commitment.

4. Your answers should conform with your answers to 3. If there is a great disparity, then you are either kidding yourself or putting up a facade. Neither condition will be useful to you as a trader.

5.d. This is the only question that has a right answer. You should use only the amount of money that, if lost, would have no impact on your financial well-being.

Practice Exam A

1. D	8. C	14. B	20. B
2. A	9. D	15. A	21. B
3. A	10. B	16. B	22. C
4. A	11. B	17. D	23. B
5. D	12. A	18. C	24. A
6. A	13. A	19. C	25. A
7. A			

Practice Exam B

1. A	8. A	15. B	21. A
2. C	9. A	16. C	22. C
3. A	10. A	17. A	23. A
4. B	11. A	18. B	24. A
5. D	12. B	19. C	25. B
6. D	13. B	20. B	26. B
7. C	14. B		

Practice Exam C

1. D	5. D	9. D
2. D	6. A	10. A
3. D	7. B	11. C
4. B	8. A	12. C

Practice Exam D

1. B	7. B	13. A	19. A
2. A	8. A	14. A	20. B
3. A	9. B	15. B	21. A
4. C	10. B	16. B	22. A
5. A	11. B	17. C	23. D
6. C	12. A	18. D	

E

FORMS USED WHEN TRADING COMMODITIES

Chicago Grain & Financial Futures Company
141 West Jackson Blvd.
Chicago, Illinois 60604

BR_____
S/S_____
CC_____

CUSTOMER AGREEMENT

Account #_____

Date_____

---

1. Name_____ Soc Sec # or Tax ID #_____ Age_____

Spouse's Name_____ Marital Status_____ No of Dependents_____

Address_____ City_____ State_____ Zip_____

Home Address (if different)_____ City_____ State_____ Zip_____

Phone (Home) (_____)_____ Phone (Business) (_____)_____ Ext_____

Employer's Name_____ Position/Title_____ Years There_____

Employer's Address_____ City_____ State_____ Zip_____

---

2. Annual Income
☐ under $40,000
☐ $40,000 to $60,000
☐ $60,000 to $90,000
☐ $90,000 to $150,000
☐ $150,000 to $400,000

Net worth excluding residence
☐ less than $50,000
☐ $50,000 to $100,000
☐ $100,000 to $200,000
☐ $200,000 to $400,000
☐ over $400,000

Total liquid Assets
$_____

Approximate Liquid Risk Capital Available_____

Bank's Name_____ Address_____ Account #_____

Bank's Name_____ Address_____ Account #_____

Other Reference_____ Address_____ Account #_____

---

3. Is Account to be directed by anyone else? ☐ yes ☐ no (if yes, Managed Account Agreement required)

If yes, by whom_____ Address_____

Is Account guaranteed by anyone else? ☐ yes ☐ no

If yes, by whom_____ Address_____

Does this account control the trading of any other account? ☐ yes ☐ no

If yes, name_____ Address_____

Does any other person have a financial interest in this account? ☐ yes ☐ no

If yes, whom_____ Address_____

Will the trading of this account be for commercial purposes? ☐ yes ☐ no

If yes, give details_____

Do you currently or did you in the past have commodity accounts with other commodity brokerage firms? ☐ yes ☐ no

If yes, Company_____ Account #_____

Have you ever had an unsecured debt at any other brokerage firm? ☐ yes ☐ no

If yes, submit details on separate sheet

Are you related to any Chicago Grain & Financial Futures employee? ☐ yes ☐ no If yes, name_____

Are you a member or employee of any commodity exchange or affiliated with any futures commission merchant or introducing broker? ☐ yes ☐ no

If yes, Please identify exchange(s) or other affiliations(s)_____

4. Indicate type of Account (check one only) ☐ Speculative or ☐ Hedging*

☐ Individual   ☐ Tenants in common (All parties must sign all forms)

☐ Partnership*   ☐ Corporate* (resolutions)

☐ Joint Tenants (All parties must sign all forms)   ☐ Managed*

*Requires additional forms

5.

Investment Experience:		Since (Year)	Transactions Per Year	Size
Stocks and Bonds	☐ yes ☐ no	_____	_____	_____
Stock Options	☐ yes ☐ no	_____	_____	_____
Mutual Funds	☐ yes ☐ no	_____	_____	_____
Limited Partnership	☐ yes ☐ no	_____	_____	_____
Commodity Futures	☐ yes ☐ no	_____	_____	_____
Managed Commodity Account	☐ yes ☐ no	_____	_____	_____

Investment Objectives: ☐ Income ☐ Growth ☐ Trading profit ☐ Speculative

How did you hear about Chicago Grain & Financial Futures?_____

Gentlemen:

In consideration of the acceptance and maintenance of one or more accounts in commodities, commodity futures contracts, options on commodities or options on commodity futures contracts (collectively, "futures contracts") by you ("Broker") for the undersigned ("Customer"), it is agreed as follows.

1. Customer authorizes Broker to purchase and sell futures contracts for Customer's account in accordance with Customer's oral or written instructions. Customer hereby waives any defense that any such instructions were not in writing as may be required by the Statute of Frauds or any other law, rule, or regulation.

2. Customer will at all times maintain collateral and margin for all accounts as from time to time may be required by Broker in its sole discretion or demanded by applicable laws or exchange regulations.

3. Customer shall pay Broker (a) applicable brokerage, commission, and other charges on any transaction executed by Broker on Customer's behalf, in effect from time to time, (b) any charges imposed on such transaction by the exchange or clearing house through which it is executed, any other transaction fees, and any tax imposed on such transaction by competent authority, (c) the amount of any trading loss suffered by Broker that may result from such transaction, and (d) interest and service charges on any deficit in Customer's account balance at the rates customarily charged by Broker, together with any costs and attorneys' fees reasonably incurred in collecting any such deficit. Such payments shall be made to Broker at its address stated above or such other place as Broker gives notice to Customer

4. All transactions by Broker on Customer's behalf shall be subject to the applicable constitution, by-laws, rules, regulations, customs, usages, rulings, and interpretations of the exchange (and its clearing house) board of trade, contract market, or other market, on which such transactions are executed or cleared by Broker or its agents for Customer's account, and to all applicable governmental acts and statutes (including, without limitation, the Commodity Exchange Act, as amended) and to the rules and regulations made by the Commodity Futures Trading Commission ("CFTC") thereunder. Broker shall not be liable to Customer as a result of any action taken by Broker or its agents to comply therewith. If any term or provision hereof, or the application thereof to any person or circumstances, shall to any extent be contrary to any law or exchange or government regulation or otherwise invalid or unenforceable, the remainder of the Agreement, or the application of such term or provision to persons or circumstances other than those as to which it is contrary, invalid or unenforceable, shall not be affected thereby, and it shall be enforced to the fullest extent permitted by regulation and law.

5. All transactions in futures contracts for or in connection with Customer's accounts shall be deemed to be included in a single account notwithstanding the fact that such transactions may be segregated on Broker's records

into separate accounts, either severally or jointly with others At any time and from time to time, in Broker's discretion. Broker may without notice to Customer, apply or transfer any or all monies. securities, commodities, options, commodities futures contracts or other property of Customer interchangeably among any of Customer's accounts, provided, however, that Broker shall not, without Customer's prior written consent use Customer s net equity in any account subject to the regulations of the CFTC under the Commodity Exchange Act, as amended. to carry trades or to offset any net deficit of Customer in goods or property not included in the term commodity as defined in said regulations.

6. Broker shall send Customer confirmation of each transaction promptly after its execution. A monthly statement of all transactions for or on behalf of Customer shall be furnished to Customer as of the last business day of each calendar month and at such other times as may be agreed upon between Broker and Customer. Confirmations of trades, statements of account, margin calls and any other notices sent by Broker to Customer shall be conclusively deemed accurate and complete if not objected to in writing within five business days from the date on which Customer receives such notice

7 In the event that (a) Customer shall fail timely to deposit or maintain or to make payment of margin or any other amount hereunder. (b) Customer (if an individual) shall die or be judicially declared incompetent or (if an entity) shall be dissolved or otherwise terminated: (c) a proceeding under the Bankruptcy Act, an assignment for the benefit of creditors, or an application for a receiver. custodian, or trustee shall be filed or applied for by or against Customer (d) an attachment is levied against Customer's account; (e) the property deposited as collateral is determined by Broker in its sole discretion, regardless of current market quotations, to be inadequate to properly secure the account. or (f) at any time Broker deems it necessary for its protection for any reason whatsoever, Broker may, in the manner it deems appropriate in order to prevent or minimize loss, close out Customer's open positions in whole or in part, sell any or all of Customer's property held by Broker, buy any securities, futures contracts, options, or other property for Customer's account, and cancel any outstanding orders and commitments made by Broker on behalf of Customer. Such sale, purchase or cancellation may be made at Broker's discretion without advertising the same and without notice to Customer or his personal representatives and without prior tender, demand for margin or payment, or call of any kind upon Customer. Broker may purchase the whole or any part thereof free from any right of redemption It is understood that a prior demand or call or prior notice of the time and place of such sale or purchase shall not be considered a wavier of Broker's right to sell or buy without demand or notice as herein provided. Customer shall remain liable for and shall pay to Broker the amount of any deficiency in any account of Customer with Broker resulting from any transaction described above.

8 Customer undertakes, at any time upon Broker's demand, to discharge all obligations to Broker, or, in the event of a closing of any of Customer's accounts in whole or in part, to pay Broker the deficiency, if any. In lieu of requiring the immediate discharge of any of Customer's obligations, Broker may, in Broker's discretion, demand security for such obligation (and, if Broker so elects, for all future obligations of Customer) in which event Customer will either discharge all existing obligations to Broker or furnish such security as Broker shall have demanded, and in that connection execute and deliver such security agreements, financing statements and other documents, in forms prescribed or approved by Broker, as Broker shall reasonably request

9 If at any time Customer fails to deliver to Broker any property previously sold by Broker on Customer's behalf or fails to deliver property, securities or financial instruments in compliance with futures contracts, or if Broker shall be required or shall deem it necessary (whether by reason of the requirements of any exchange, clearing house or otherwise) to replace any securities, futures contracts, financial instruments or other property theretofore delivered by Broker for the account of Customer with other property of like or equivalent kind or amount. Customer authorizes Broker in its judgment to borrow or to buy any property necessary to make delivery thereof or to replace any such property previously delivered and to deliver the same to such other party to whom delivery is to be made. Broker may subsequently repay any borrowing thereof with property purchased or otherwise acquired for the account of Customer. Customer shall pay Broker for any cost, loss and damage from the foregoing (including consequential damages, penalties and fines) which Broker may be required to incur or which Broker may sustain from its inability to borrow or buy any such property

10 All monies, securities, options, financial instruments, futures contracts or other property ("property") now or at any future time in Customer's account or held for Customer (either individually or jointly with others) by Broker or by any clearing house through which Customer's trades are executed, or which may be in Broker's possession for any purpose (including safekeeping) are hereby pledged with Broker and shall be subject to a security interest and general lien in Broker's favor to secure all indebtedness at any time owing from Customer to Broker. Broker is hereby authorized to sell any and all property in any of Customer's accounts without notice to satisfy such general lien

11 All property now or hereafter held or carried by Broker for Customer may from time to time without notice to Customer be invested by Broker or others, separately or with any other property, provided that such property shall be segregated to the extent required by, and shall be invested only in accordance with, rules of the CFTC. Broker shall be under no obligation to deliver the same certificates, instruments or securities deposited with Broker or received by Broker for the account of Customer but may deliver other certificates, instruments or securities of like or equivalent kind or amount

12 Customer consents to transactions with other customers of Broker, including affiliates of Broker, as long as they are executed at prevailing prices in the manner provided for on the exchange where the futures contract is traded. Customer understands that Broker or any of its affiliates may have a position in and may buy or sell futures contracts which are the subject of information or recommendations furnished to Customer. Broker makes no representation, warranty, or guarantee with respect to the tax consequences of Customer's transactions

13 Broker shall not be liable for delays in the transmission or execution of orders due to breakdown or failure of transmission or communication facilities, or for any other cause beyond Broker's control

14 Customer acknowledges that any trading recommendations and market or other information communicated to Customer by Broker do not constitute an offer to sell or the solicitation of an offer to buy any futures contract. Any such recommendations and information, although based upon information obtained from sources believed by Broker to be reliable, may be incomplete, may not be verified and may be changed without notice to Customer, and Broker makes no representation, warranty or guarantee with respect thereto

15 All communications to Customer shall be to his mailing address indicated below or to such other place as Customer gives notice in writing to Broker. All communications so sent to Customer, whether by mail, telegraph, messenger or otherwise, shall be deemed to have been personally delivered to Customer, whether actually received or not. Notices sent by messenger shall be deemed duly given when delivered to the address of Customer as designated below. Notices sent by telegraph shall be deemed duly given one hour after the time of receipt by the telegraph office. Notices sent by mail shall be deemed duly given at 9 00 A M (Chicago time) on the business day immediately following the date of mailing. All communications to Broker shall be to its address stated above or such other place as Broker gives notice to Customer

16 The rights and remedies conferred upon Broker shall be cumulative, and the exercise or waiver of any thereof shall not preclude or inhibit the exercise of additional rights and remedies. Broker's failure at any time to insist upon strict compliance with this Agreement or any of its terms or any continued course of such conduct on Customer's part shall not constitute or be considered a waiver by Broker of any of its rights. This Agreement contains the entire agreement between the parties and supersedes any prior agreements between the parties as to the subject matter of this Agreement. Subject to section 4 hereof, no provision of this Agreement shall in any respect be waived, modified, altered, or changed except in a writing signed by a duly authorized officer of Broker. This Agreement shall be construed according to and the rights and liabilities of the parties hereto shall be governed by the laws of the State of Illinois

17 This Agreement shall inure to the benefit of the Broker, its successors and assigns and shall be binding upon Customer and Customer's heirs, estate, executors, administrators, successors and assigns. The provisions of this Agreement shall be continuous and shall cover individually and collectively all accounts which Customer now maintains or may in the future open or reopen with Broker

18 Customer represents that (a) (if an individual), he is of the age of majority of sound mind, and authorized to open accounts and enter into this Agreement and to effectuate transactions in futures contracts as contemplated hereby. (b) if an entity, Customer is validly existing and empowered to enter into this Agreement and to effect transactions in futures contracts as contemplated hereby. (c) the statements and financial information contained on Customer's Application submitted herewith (including any financial statement submitted therewith) are true and correct. (d) Customer has read, understands and has signed the CFTC Risk Disclosure Statements previously furnished by Broker, and (e) no person or entity has any interest in or control of the account to which this Agreement pertains except as disclosed in the Customer's Application. Customer further represents that, except as heretofore disclosed to Broker in writing, he is not an officer or employee of any exchange, board of trade, clearing house, bank or trust company or an "affiliated person" (as defined in the regulations of the CFTC) of any futures commission merchant, or an introducing broker, or an officer, partner, director, or employee of any securities broker or dealer. Customer agrees to furnish supplemental financial statements to Broker, to disclose to Broker any material changes in the financial position of Customer and to furnish promptly such other information concerning Customer as Broker reasonably requests

19 Customer affirms that he is able to assume the financial risks of commodity futures trading and that commodity futures trading meets his financial objectives. Customer agrees to notify Broker if there is any material change in his financial condition or objectives

20 Customer is aware that commodity futures trading is a highly speculative activity and that commodity futures are purchased on small margins and are subject to sharp price movements. Customer understands that on days on which a commodity futures contract is up or down its permissable exchange price limit, Customer may be unable to close out his position in that contract. Customer also realizes, because of the relatively small margins required, that he may be risking more than any sums or property deposited with Broker and that significant losses could be suffered

21 Customer understands that an investigation may be made pertaining to his credit standing and his business accounts, and authorizes Broker to contact such banks, financial institutions, and credit agencies as broker shall deem appropriate

22 Customer acknowledges Broker's right to limit the number of open positions which Customer may maintain or acquire through Broker at any time and Customer agrees not to make any trade through Broker which would have the effect of exceeding the limitations imposed on Customer by Broker. Customer further agrees not to exceed the position limits set by the CFTC or any exchange, whether acting alone or with others, and to promptly advise Broker if Customer is required to file reports or commodity positions with the CFTC

23 Customer understands that Broker in its sole discretion may record, on tape or otherwise, any telephone conversation between Broker and Customer. Customer hereby agrees and consents to such recording and waives any right Customer may have to object to the admissibility into evidence of such recording in any legal proceeding between Customer and Broker or in any other proceeding to which Broker is a party on in which Broker's records are subpoenaed

(Over for Signature)

24 If Customer's account is carried by Broker only as a clearing broker. Customer acknowledges that Broker is not responsible for the conduct. representations, and statements of the introducing broker in the handling of Customer's account.

25 Where the context requires. the singular shall import the plural and the masculine shall import the feminine

Dated_____

x_____

Customer's Signature

x_____

If this is a joint account, all persons must sign

RISK DISCLOSURE STATEMENT FOR NON-CASH MARGIN THIS STATEMENT IS FURNISHED TO YOU BECAUSE RULE 190 10 (C) OF THE COMMODITY FUTURES TRADING COMMISSION REQUIRES IT FOR REASONS OF FAIR NOTICE UNRELATED TO THIS COMPANY'S CURRENT FINANCIAL CONDITION. 1 YOU SHOULD KNOW THAT IN THE UNLIKELY EVENT OF THIS COMPANY'S BANKRUPTCY. PROPERTY. INCLUDING PROPERTY SPECIFICALLY TRACEABLE TO YOU. WILL BE RETURNED. TRANSFERRED OR DISTRIBUTED TO YOU. OR ON YOUR BEHALF. ONLY TO THE EXTENT OF YOUR PRO RATA SHARE OF ALL PROPERTY AVAILABLE FOR DISTRIBUTION TO CUSTOMERS 2 NOTICE CONCERNING THE TERMS FOR THE RETURN OF SPECIFICALLY IDENTIFIABLE PROPERTY WILL BE BY PUBLICATION IN A NEWSPAPER OF GENERAL CIRCULATION 3. THE COMMISSION'S REGULATIONS CONCERNING BANKRUPTCIES OF COMMODITY BROKERS CAN BE FOUND AT 17 CODE OF FEDERAL REGULATIONS PART 190

Acknowledgment I hereby acknowledge that I reviewed the foregoing Risk Disclosure Statement on the date indicated below and that I fully understand its contents.

Dated: _____

x_____

x_____

(Customer's Signature (s)

LOAN CONSENT Subject to the provisions of the Commodity Exchange Act. and any applicable CFTC or exchange regulations. Broker is hereby specifically authorized to lend to itself or to others, or to rehypothecate any securities held by Broker for any accounts of the undersigned until Broker receives written notice of revocation signed by the undersigned.

Dated:_____

x_____

x_____

Customer's Signature(s)

CONSENT TO JURISDICTION The parties agree that all disputes, claims, actions or proceedings arising directly, indirectly or otherwise in connection with. out of, related to or from this Customer Agreement and any related agreement shall be litigated at the discretion and election of Chicago Grain and Financial Futures Company ("Chicago Grain") only in a court in Chicago, Illinois. The undersigned customer ("Customer") consents and submits to the jurisdiction of any state or federal court located within the City of Chicago. State of Illinois. appoints and designates Chicago Grain (or any other party whom Chicago Grain may from time to time hereinafter designate) as Customer's true and lawful attorney-in-fact and duly authorized agent for service of legal process. and agrees that service of such process upon Chicago Grain or such other party shall constitute personal service of such process upon Customer. provided that Chicago Grain or such other party shall, within five days after receipt of any such process, forward the same by certified or registered mail. together with all papers affixed thereto, to Customer at Customer's mailing address. Customer hereby waives any right Customer may have to transfer or change the venue of any litigation brought against Customer by Chicago Grain.

x_____

Dated:_____

x_____

Customer's Signature(s)

Make all checks payable to Chicago Grain & Financial Futures Company
To bank wire funds. Continental Illinois National Bank
231 South LaSalle St.
Chicago, IL 60604
For the account of
Chicago Grain & Financial Futures
Customers Segregated Account
#72-11082

When wiring funds please include name. account number, and name of the Agent or Introducing Broker you deal through

In order for account to be processed, all sections and Risk Disclosure Statements must be signed by all parties.

APPROVED BY:
ASSOCIATED PERSON

_____DATE_____

DESIGNATED SUPERVISOR

_____DATE_____

OFFICER

_____DATE_____

RISK DISCLOSURE STATEMENTS
FURNISHED ON_____

OPTIONS DISCLOSURE STATEMENT
FURNISHED ON_____

Grain & Financial Futures Company

RISK DISCLOSURE STATEMENT

141 West Jackson Boulevard
Chicago, Illinois 60604

Account No._____

RISK DISCLOSURE STATEMENT

This statement is furnished to you because rule 1.55 of the Commodity Futures Trading Commission requires it.

The risk of loss in trading commodity futures contracts can be substantial. You should therefore carefully consider whether such trading is suitable for you in light of your financial condition. In considering whether to trade, you should be aware of the following:

(1) You may sustain a total loss of the initial margin funds and any additional funds that you deposit with your broker to establish or maintain a position in the commodity futures market. If the market moves against your position, you may be called upon by your broker to deposit a substantial amount of additional margin funds, on short notice, in order to maintain your position. If you do not provide the required funds within the prescribed time, your position may be liquidated at a loss, and you will be liable for any resulting deficit in your account.

(2) Under certain market conditions, you may find it difficult or impossible to liquidate a position. This can occur, for example, when the market makes a "limit move."

(3) Placing contingent orders, such as a "stop-loss" or a "stop-limit" order, will not necessarily limit your losses to the intended amounts, since market conditions may make it impossible to execute such orders.

(4) A "spread" position may not be less risky than a simple "long" or "short" position.

(5) The high degree of leverage that is often obtainable in futures trading because of the small margin requirements can work against you as well as for you. The use of leverage can lead to large losses as well as gains.

This brief statement cannot, of course, disclose all the risks and other significant aspects of the commodity markets. You should therefore carefully study futures trading before you trade.

Acknowledgement of Receipt

I hereby acknowledge that I received a copy of this Risk Disclosure Statement from Chicago Grain and Financial Futures Company on the date indicated below, and that I fully understand its contents.

Date:_____, 19____

_____
Signature of Customer

_____
Signature of Customer

Sign and return first copy.
For your records, sign and keep the bottom copy.

HEDGING AGREEMENT

Chicago Grain and Financial
  Futures Company
141 West Jackson Boulevard
Chicago, Illinois 60604

Gentlemen:

1. Unless specified in writing to the contrary, all orders for the purchase or sale of futures contracts for the account indicated below will represent "hedging" transactions and positions as defined in Section 1.3(z) of the Regulations of the Commodity Futures Trading Commission ("CFTC"), as such regulations currently exist or may hereafter be amended. Should I give orders for the purchase or sale of futures contracts that do not meet the definition of "hedging", I shall advise you in writing to that effect and will keep these and other contracts margined as required by you and the applicable contract market rules.

2. I understand that the CFTC requires you to solicit certain information from me with respect to the disposition of open contracts in this hedging account in the unlikely event of the insolvency of your firm. Specifically, CFTC Rule 190.06(d) requires that I indicate whether open commodity contracts held in this account are to be liquidated by any appointed bankruptcy trustee, without further instructions from me, in the event of your firm's insolvency. In such event, open commodity contracts held in the undersigned's hedging account should be handled as follows:

[Check One Box]

☐   Liquidated by the bankruptcy trustee without seeking
         further instructions from the undersigned.

☐   Seek further instructions from the undersigned regard-
         ing liquidation or transfer.

These directions shall remain in effect until revoked in writing.

_____

_____
Signature(s) of Customer

Dated: _____

Account No.   _____

Chicago Grain & Financial
Futures Company

ACCOUNT TRANSFER FORM

Suite 2706
141 West Jackson Boulevard
Chicago, Illinois 60604
312/427-9033

**Please Complete and Return With Your
New Account Forms to
Chicago Grain & Financial Futures Company**

Your Name _____
Address _____
City, State, Zip _____
Date _____

Current Brokerage House

To _____
_____
_____ Account # _____

Dear Sir:

I have this day given to Chicago Grain & Financial Futures Company this form and my permission for them to present it to you at their discretion. In accordance with the Commodity Futures Trading Commission Act, I hereby request that upon presentation to you by Chicago Grain & Financial Futures Company you do the following:

Immediately transfer my account balance, any open positions, margins or securities to CHICAGO GRAIN & FINANCIAL FUTURES COMPANY, 141 W. Jackson Boulevard, Suite #2706, Chicago, Illinois 60604, sending me a confirmation of this transfer.

Sincerely,

_____
Signature

222 S. Riverside Plaza, Suite 414, Chicago IL 60606, 800/621-3106, IL 312/454-9502

Chicago Grain & Financial Futures Company

141 West Jackson Boulevard
Chicago, Illinois 60604

Gentlemen:

The undersigned hereby authorizes _____

_____ (the "Agent") whose

address is _____, to buy,

sell (including short sales), transfer, trade, and otherwise deal in: (a) commodity futures contracts; (b) options on commodity futures contract; (c) commodities; all in his sole discretion, for my account no. _____ with you and in my name. I understand that all such activity by the Agent will be subject to all rules and regulations, and all amendments thereto, by which you are governed.

In all such transactions, you are authorized to follow the instructions of the Agent in every respect concerning my account with you; and, except as otherwise provided herein, the Agent is authorized to act with full power and authority for me and in my behalf in the same manner and with the same force and effect as I might or could do if personally present with respect to such transactions as well as with respect to all other things necessary or incidental to the furtherance or conduct of such transactions, except that the Agent is not authorized to withdraw any money, securities, or other property in the name of the undersigned or otherwise. The Agent shall specifically designate all such transactions as being made pursuant to the authority granted hereunder.

I agree that you shall have no liability for following the instructions of the Agent; and I further agree never to attempt to hold you liable for the Agent's actions. I hereby release you from any and all liability to me or anyone claiming through me with respect to any damage, losses or lost profits sustained or alleged to have been sustained as a result of your following the Agent's instructions. I further agree to pay any debit balance on my account and to promptly meet all margin requirements, whether or not incurred for me as a result of the Agent's instructions. This authorization and indemnity is in addition to, and in no way limits or restricts, any rights which you may have under any other agreement or agreements between you and the undersigned.

I hereby ratify and confirm any and all transactions with you heretofore or hereafter made by the Agent for my account.

This Trading Authorization will not terminate unless revoked by written notice by the undersigned addressed to you and delivered to your office at 141 West Jackson Boulevard, Chicago, Illinois 60604, but such revocation shall not affect any liability in any way resulting from transactions initiated prior to such revocation. The authorization and indemnity contained herein shall inure to the benefit of your present firm and of any successor firm or firms, irrespective of any change or changes at any time in the personnel thereof for any cause whatsoever, and of the assigns of your present firm or any successor firm.

I have carefully examined the provisions of this Trading Authorization by which I have given trading authority or control over my account to the Agent and understand the obligations which I have assumed by executing this document.

I understand that your firm is in no way responsible for any loss to me occasioned by the Agent and that your firm does not, by implication or otherwise, endorse the operating method of the agent. I further understand that the Chicago Board of Trade and the Chicago Mercantile Exchange have no jurisdiction over a non-member who is not employed by one of their members and that if I give to such an individual or organization authority to exercise any of my rights over my account, I do so at my own risk.

Very truly yours,

Dated: _____   _____

                                          _____

                                          [Name of Account Holder]
                                          (If more than one, all
                                          principals to the Account
                                          must sign.)

Acknowledged:

_____

Agent

Chicago Grain & Financial Futures Company

141 West Jackson Blvd
Chicago, Illinois 60604

Account No. _____

PARTNERSHIP ACCOUNT AGREEMENT

The undersigned

_____   _____
(NAME)   (ADDRESS)

_____   _____
(NAME)   (ADDRESS)

_____   _____
(NAME)   (ADDRESS)

_____   _____
(NAME)   (ADDRESS)

Being all of the partners doing business under the firm name and style of _____

_____ , with offices at _____
in consideration of your carrying their partnership, account, agree that:

1. Any one or more of the undersigned shall have full authority for the account and risk and in the name of said partnership, through you as our brokers.

   (a) To buy, sell and trade in commodities for present or future delivery, on margin or otherwise, the power to sell including the power to sell "short";

   (b) To deposit with and withdraw from your firm money, commodities, contracts for purchase or sale of commodities, checks and other negotiable instruments, securities and other property, including withdrawals to or for the individual use of account of the partner directing the sale or of any other partner;

   (c) To receive and acquiesce in the correctness of notices, confirmations, requests, demands and communications of every kind;

   (d) To settle, compromise, adjust and give releases with respect to any and all claims, demands, disputes and controversies;

   (e) To make agreements and take any other action relating to any of the foregoing matters.

   This enumeration of specific authority shall not in any way limit or affect any other authority which any partner of our firm might otherwise have.

2. Each partner will enter into a customer agreement and other necessary forms with the firm no later than the first day on which a purchase or sale is made for the partnership.

3. The undersigned are jointly and severally liable to your firm for any and all obligations arising out of transactions herein authorized.

4. Any and all past transactions of any kind herein authorized which may have been heretofore had by any one or more of the undersigned through or with your firm are hereby ratified.

5. Upon death of any of the undersigned, you are authorized to take such action in regard to our account as you may deem advisable to protect you against any liability, penalty or loss. We agree to notify you immediately upon the death of any undersigned.

6. The authority herein granted is in addition to any other authority given to you by any or all of the undersigned and is a continuing one and shall remain in full force and effect until your firm shall receive at its offices written notice of revocation or modification hereof.

7. Your firm may terminate this agreement by written notice to any of the above partners.

WITNESS:

_____   _____

_____   _____

(Original)
Please sign and return.

Grain & Financial
Futures Company

141 West Jackson Blvd
Chicago. Illinois 60604

CORPORATION ACCOUNT
(AUTHORIZING TRADING IN COMMODITIES)

Gentlemen:

The undersigned Corporation, by_____ its President,
pursuant to the resolutions a copy of which, certified by the Secretary, is annexed hereto, hereby
authorizes you to open an account in the name of said Corporation; and the undersigned also
encloses herewith your Customer's Agreement duly executed on behalf of the Corporation. This
authorization shall continue in force until revoked by the undersigned Corporation by a written
notice, addressed to you and delivered at your office at

Dated,_____

_____
            (City)   (State)

                              Very truly yours,

                              _____

                         By_____
                                                  President

I,_____ , being the Secretary of_____
_____ , hereby certify that the annexed resolutions were duly adopted at a
meeting of the Board of Directors of said Corporation, duly held on the _____
day of_____ , at which a quorum of said Board of Directors was present and
acting throughout and that no action has been taken to rescind or amend said resolutions and that
the same are now in full force and effect.

I further certify that each of the following has been duly elected and is now legally holding the
office set opposite his name:

                              , President
                              , Vice-President
                              , Treasurer
                              , Secretary

I further certify that the said Corporation is duly organized and existing and has the power to
take the action called for by the resolutions annexed hereto.

IN WITNESS WHEREOF, I have hereunto affixed my hand this_____day of
_____ , 19___.

                              _____
                                                  Secretary

CERTIFIED COPY OF CERTAIN RESOLUTIONS ADOPTED BY THE BOARD OF DIRECTORS WHEREBY THE ESTABLISHMENT AND MAINTENANCE OF TRADING ACCOUNTS HAVE BEEN AUTHORIZED

RESOLVED—

FIRST: That the President or any Vice President of this Corporation, or   or
                                    be and they hereby are, and each of them hereby is, authorized and empowered, for and on behalf of this Corporation (herein called the "Corporation"), to establish and maintain one or more accounts, which may be marginal accounts, with
(herein called the "Brokers") for the purpose of purchasing, investing in, or otherwise acquiring, selling (including short-sales), possessing, transferring, exchanging, pledging, or otherwise disposing of, or turning to account of, or realizing upon, and generally dealing in and with any and all commodities and/or contracts for the future delivery thereof, whether represented by trust, participating and/or other certificates or otherwise.

The fullest authority at all times with respect to any such commitment or with respect to any transaction deemed by any of the said officers and/or agents to be proper in connection therewith is hereby conferred, including authority (without limiting the generality of the foregoing) to give written or oral instructions to the Brokers with respect to said transactions, to borrow money, securities, commodities and/or future contracts in commodities, and to borrow such money, securities, commodities and/or future contracts in commodities from or through the Brokers, and to secure repayment thereof with the property of the Corporation; to bind and obligate the Corporation to and for the carrying out of any contract, arrangement, or transaction, which shall be entered into by any such officer and/or agent for and on behalf of the Corporation with or through the Brokers; to pay in cash or by checks and/or drafts drawn upon the funds of the Corporation such sums as may be necessary in connection with any of the said accounts; to deliver securities, contracts and/or commodity futures to the Brokers, to order the transfer or delivery thereof to any other person whatsoever, and/or to order the transfer of record of any securities, or contracts, or titles, to any name selected by any of the said officers or agents; to affix the corporate seal to any documents or agreements, or otherwise; to endorse any securities and/or contracts in order to pass title thereto; to direct the sale or exercise of any rights with respect to any securities; to sign for the Corporation all releases, powers of attorney and/or other documents in connection with any such account, and to agree to any terms or conditions to control any such account; to direct the Brokers to surrender any securities to the proper agent or party for the purpose of effecting any exchange or conversion, or for the purpose of deposit with any protective or similar committee, or otherwise; to accept delivery of any securities, contracts and/or commodity futures; to appoint any other person or persons to do any and all things which any of the said officers and/or agents is hereby empowered to do and generally to do and take all action necessary in connection with the account, or considered desirable by such officer and/or agent with respect thereto.

SECOND: That the Brokers may deal with any and all of the persons directly or indirectly by the foregoing resolution empowered, as though they were dealing with the Corporation directly.

THIRD: That the Secretary of the Corporation be and he hereby is authorized, empowered and directed to certify, under the seal of the Corporation, or otherwise, to the Brokers:

(a) a true copy of these resolutions;

(b) specimen signatures of each and every person by these resolutions empowered;

(c) a certificate (which, if required by the Brokers, shall be supported by an opinion of the general counsel of the Corporation, or other counsel satisfactory to the Brokers) that the Corporation is duly organized and existing, that its charter empowers it to transact the business by these resolutions defined, and that no limitation has been imposed upon such powers by the By-Laws or otherwise.

FOURTH: That the Brokers may rely upon any certification given in accordance with these resolutions, as continuing fully effective unless and until the Brokers shall receive due written notice of a change in or the rescission of the authority so evidenced and the dispatch or receipt of any other form of notice shall not constitute a waiver of this provision, nor shall the fact that any person hereby empowered ceases to be an officer of the Corporation or becomes an officer under some other title in any way affect the powers hereby conferred. The failure to supply any specimen signature shall not invalidate any transaction if the transaction is in accordance with authority actually granted.

-2-

FIFTH: That in the event of any change in the office or powers or persons hereby empowered, the Secretary shall certify such changes to the Brokers in writing in the manner hereinabove provided, which notification, when received, shall be adequate both to terminate the powers of the persons theretofore authorized, and to empower the persons thereby substituted.

SIXTH: That the foregoing resolutions and the certificates actually furnished to the Brokers by the Secretary of the Corporation pursuant thereto, be and they hereby are made irrevocable until written notice of the revocation thereof shall have been received by the Brokers.

SEVENTH: That the following persons not heretofore stated are empowered to transmit and receive orders for the account of the Corporation.

Name _____ Title _____

Name _____ Title _____

Name _____ Title _____

Name _____ Title _____

INDEX